D0466570

# COLIN MAGGS'S
# WEST OF ENGLAND

## BROAD-GAUGE FAREWELL

### *Horatio F. Brown*

So! I shall never see you more,
You mighty lord of railway-roar;
The splendid stroke of driving-wheel,
The burnished brass, the shining steel,
Triumphant pride of him who drives
From Paddington to far St Ives.
Another year, and then your place
Knows you no more; a pigmy race
Usurps the glory of the road,
And trails along a lesser load.
Drive on then, engine, drive amain,
Wrap me, like love, yet once again,
A follower in your fiery train.

Drive on! and driving, let me know
The golden West, its warmth, its glow.
Pass Thames with all his winding maze;
Sweet Clifton dreaming in a haze;
And, farther yet, pass Taunton Vale,
And Dawlish rocks, and Teignmouth sail,
And Totnes, where the dancing Dart
Comes seaward with a gladsome heart;
Then let me feel the wind blow free
From levels of the Cornish sea.

Drive on! let all you fiery soul,
Your puissant heart that scorns control,
Your burnished limbs of circling steel,
The throb, the pulse of driving-wheel,
O'erflood the breast of him whose gaze
Is set to watch your perilous ways. . . .

# COLIN MAGGS'S WEST OF ENGLAND

Colin G. Maggs

SUTTON PUBLISHING

First published in the United Kingdom in 1998
Sutton Publishing Limited · Phoenix Mill · Far Thrupp · Stroud · Gloucestershire

British Library Cataloguing in Publication Data

A catalogue record for this book is available from the British Library.

ISBN 0 7509 1618 4

*Jacket pictures: Front, '72XX' class 2–8–2T No. 7250 leaves the picturesque portal of Twerton tunnel with a Down permanent way train carrying rails, 30.7.63 (Author); Back, top to bottom, 'West Country' class Pacific No. 34003* Plymouth *near Semley with the 12.56 p.m. Salisbury–Yeovil Town, 4.8.62 (Author); '64XX' class 0–6–0PT No. 6412 at Buckfastleigh on the South Devon Railway sandwiched between two pairs of auto trailers – Easter 1970 (W.H. Harbor); visiting '1336' class 0–6–0PT No. 1369, allocated to Wadebridge shed in the 1960s for use on the Wenford Bridge branch, is seen here at Boscarne Junction on the Bodmin & Wenford Railway, heading a reproduction china clay train, September 1996 (Brian Aston).*

 ALAN SUTTON™ and SUTTON™ are the trade marks of Sutton Publishing Limited

Typeset in Bembo 11/13 pt.
Typesetting and origination by
Sutton Publishing Limited.
Printed in Great Britain by
Butler & Tanner, Frome, Somerset.

# CONTENTS

Map of Railways in the West of England ........................................................vi

Preface ............................................................................................................viii

Railways in the West of England

    Early Railways ..........................................................................................1

    Gauge Conversion ....................................................................................2

    Freight Yesterday and Today....................................................................6

    Passenger Traffic Yesterday and Today ..................................................15

    Railway Docks and Steamer Services ......................................................17

    Railway Architecture ..............................................................................20

    Locomotives ............................................................................................30

    Main Line Internal Combustion Engined Power ..................................63

    Concrete Depots ....................................................................................68

    Railway Buses..........................................................................................69

    Road Transport for Goods ....................................................................72

    Railway Air Services................................................................................73

    Preserved Railways ................................................................................75

Main Lines: GWR ........................................................................................81

Branch Lines: GWR ....................................................................................114

Main Lines: LSWR/SR ................................................................................136

Branch Lines: LSWR/SR ............................................................................165

Select Bibliography ......................................................................................184

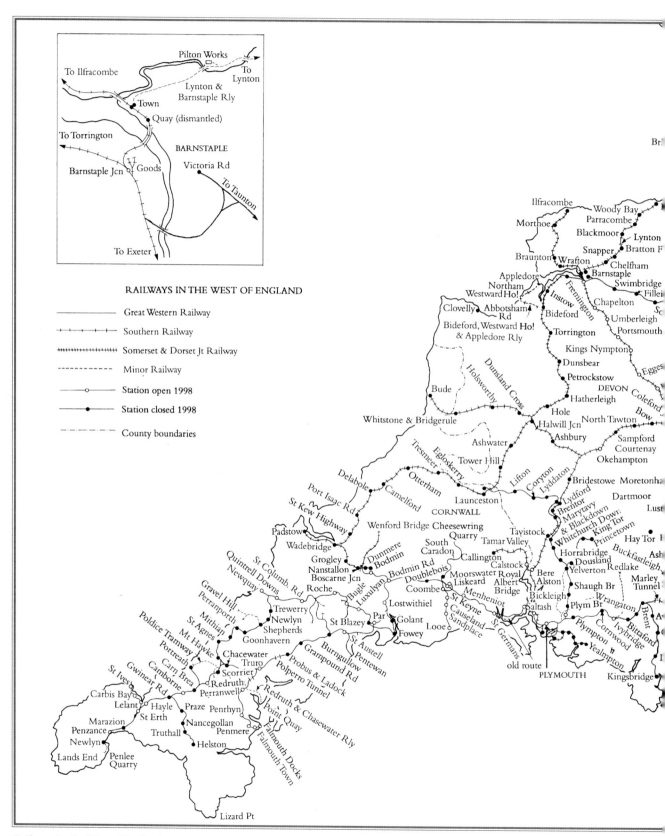

## Inset map (Barnstaple)

To Ilfracombe

Pilton Works

To Lynton

Town

Lynton & Barnstaple Rly

Quay (dismantled)

To Torrington

BARNSTAPLE

Barnstaple Jcn — Goods

Victoria Rd

To Taunton

To Exeter

## RAILWAYS IN THE WEST OF ENGLAND

———————— Great Western Railway

+—+—+—+—+ Southern Railway

++++++++++++ Somerset & Dorset Jt Railway

-------- Minor Railway

—o— Station open 1998

—•— Station closed 1998

– – – County boundaries

Railways in the West of England

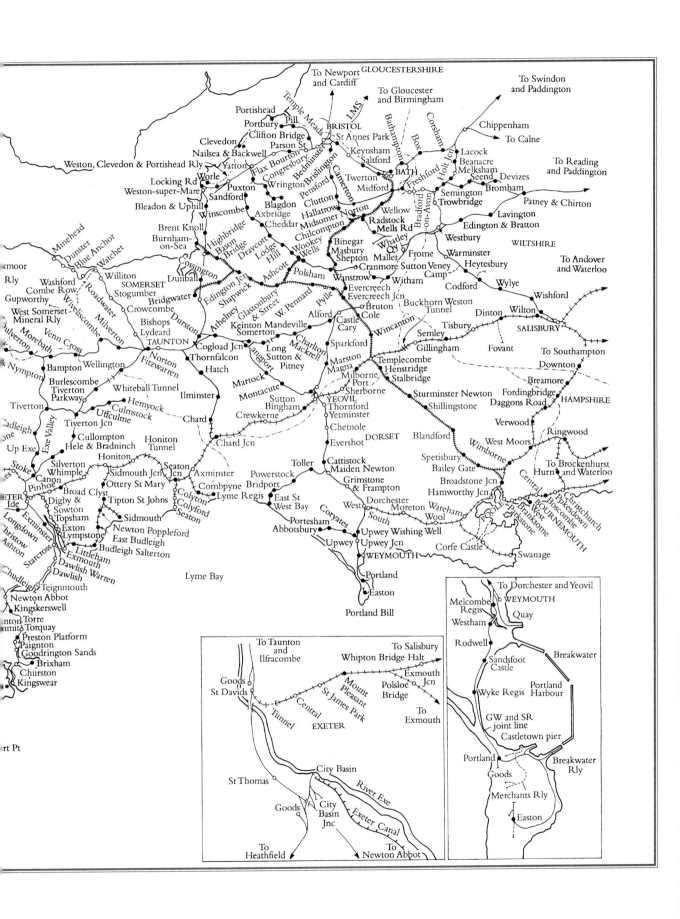

# PREFACE

What picture springs to your mind when hearing the words 'West of England'? Is it of an idyllic branch line twisting along the floor of a lush green valley? Or perhaps you think of a holiday express proceeding swiftly along a main line, or pounding up a fearsome gradient? Is the image that of a complete train in eye-catching malachite green, or a dark-green engine hauling tea and cream-coloured coaches? Or could that train be carrying clay, strawberries, early vegetables, coal, petrol, oil, milk or cattle?

The aim of this book is to provide a general picture of railways in the West of England – from the beginning right up to the present day. The 'West of England' is considered here to comprise Cornwall, Devon, Dorset, Somerset and south-west Wiltshire. It does not claim to cover the whole of this area in detail and photographs have a bias towards the 1950–68 period, the years most familiar to readers.

Grateful thanks are due to E.J.M. Hayward for checking and improving the text and captions.

# RAILWAYS IN THE WEST OF ENGLAND

## EARLY RAILWAYS

The West of England was the cradle of railways in Britain. Early in the eighteenth century Ralph Allen purchased the right to quarry stone on Combe Down, near Bath. Possessing good business acumen, he realized that in order to make a reasonable profit, a way had to be devised for transporting large blocks of stone, weighing upwards of 4 tons, from his quarry to a wharf he had built on the River Avon 1½ miles distant and 500 ft below. There the stone could be sold to builders who were rapidly expanding Bath, or shipped down the Avon to Bristol and then taken onwards to Dublin and Belfast, thereby breaking the monopoly of Portland stone. As the state of the roads made transport by traditional sledge or cart impracticable, Allen's solution was a railway. It was not quite a novel idea as he had seen railways in Northumberland while on his travels in connection with the postal service.

On a gradient of 1 in 10, the timber rails, probably of oak, were set to a gauge of 3 ft 9 in. The wagons, also of oak, had low detachable sides and short upright ends. The precursors of modern low-sided goods wagons, they ran on four cast-iron spoked wheels with deep flanges, the latter being an innovation as hitherto the rails, not wheels, had been flanged. Two horses drew trucks on level ground, or an empty wagon uphill, but loaded vehicles descended by gravity and an efficient braking system was provided. The railway opened in 1731 enabling stone to be delivered at the wharf for 7s 6d a ton – a worthwhile reduction on the previous cost of 10s. Later, rails were laid on the north side of the river and loaded trucks were carried across on barges – Allen had invented the train ferry. He died on 29 June 1764 and shortly after the railway was dismantled. The idea was not forgotten and some thirty years later when the Kennet & Avon Canal was cut, double-acting inclines were built linking various quarries with the waterway.

Another early line was the Haytor Tramway. It opened on 16 September 1820 and carried granite from Haytor, on Dartmoor, to north of Teigngrace where the stone was transhipped to a barge on the Stover Canal before transference to a sea-going vessel at Teignmouth. The rarity of the line was that its rails were of granite and set at a gauge of 4 ft 3 in. Parts of the tramway can still be followed today and it has rightly been scheduled an Ancient Monument. Haytor granite was used for constructing the British Museum, the National Gallery and London Bridge, but eventually granite was obtained from cheaper sources and in 1858 the tramway fell into disuse.

Other early lines were the Plymouth & Dartmoor Railway which opened its 23 miles of 4 ft 6 in gauge from Sutton Pool, Plymouth to King Tor on 26 September 1823, while the Lee Moor Tramway, to the same gauge, until closure in 1961 still had its horse-worked rail level crossing at Laira Junction across the BR main line to the west.

A glance at a railway map of the West of England shows that in the days before the 1923 grouping the GWR and the LSWR were the predominant companies. Both thrust lines westwards from London to Exeter and Plymouth, the GWR alone extending to Penzance. Both companies threw branches to places off the main line, the LSWR seizing South-east and North Devon, leaving South Devon and most of Cornwall, except the North, to the GWR.

## GAUGE CONVERSION

The GWR and its allies favoured the broad gauge of 7 ft 0¼ in, but the LSWR used the 4 ft 8½ in standard gauge. Differences in gauge were of little consequence in the early days when each line was an entity in itself, but as the network expanded, differences in gauge obstructed through running, necessitating the time and expense of transhipment. There were some advantages in retaining the broad gauge. For example, when in 1878 the Bristol & Exeter Railway decided to convert its branches to standard gauge, it purposely retained broad gauge on the Chard branch for as long as possible in order to prevent the LSWR from obtaining running powers to Taunton. It was converted eventually on 19 July 1891, only ten months prior to the final conversion of the GWR broad gauge lines in May 1892, the 105½ miles of track between Exeter and Truro being the major length requiring alteration, as Truro to Penzance was already mixed gauge.

The tremendous task of conversion was organized with military precision. No goods traffic was despatched to the area after 17 May; on 18 and 19 May trains brought 3,400 men to reinforce the local permanent way staff. The *Western Morning News* reported:

> The men will not expect any sumptuous preparations for their comfort and they will not be disappointed. Where neither stations or other buildings are available, the men will sleep in tents. For sleeping purposes, each man will have a canvas bag stuffed with straw, and for covering, a couple of rugs. Every man will provide his own food, and in the vicinity of towns and villages, bakers will be prepared to supply their wants. After work from morning till night, the men will be so tired that they will be quite willing to make shift with the only possible accommodation that could be provided. The work will be done without the oft-boasted aid of alcohol, as has been the case at previous conversions. After work is over each day, the inspectors will not be called upon to prevent the men obtaining intoxicants. During worktime however, the workmen will be refreshed with oatmeal water, made palatable with sugar. For this purpose the company have supplied ten tons of oatmeal. The well-known tobacco manufacturer of Bristol, Messrs W.D. & H.O. Wills, one of the partners of which firm is a director of the Great Western Railway, have shown a kindly thoughtfulness which almost exceeds their generosity. They have forwarded for the consumption by men, 5,000 2 oz packets of their famous Westward Ho! mixture. This gift represents over £150. The tobacco will be distributed amongst the men. Who can doubt their appreciation of this act?

Men working on the conversion were paid 25 per cent more than their regular wage as well as a shilling for each night spent away from home. The 4,200 men were placed in gangs of twenty and required to convert just over a mile of track.

The mixed gauge track can be clearly seen in this view of a 'Rover' class 4–2–2 heading a Down train through Stoke Canon station in May 1891. The platforms were staggered either side of a level crossing. This station closed on 1 July 1894 and was replaced by another 500 yds to the south and sited immediately before the junction of the Exe Valley Branch.

May 1891 Author's collection

The last Up broad gauge train stands at Truro headed by two convertible engines: '1076' class 0–6–0ST No. 1256, built as a standard gauge engine in 1877, converted to broad gauge in 1887, back to standard gauge in 1892 and withdrawn in 1936; '3521' class 0–4–4T No. 3557, built in 1889 as an 0–4–2ST but ran so unsteadily that in 1891 short side and back tanks replaced its saddle and a trailing bogie was fitted. Converted to standard gauge in 1892, it still suffered from unsteadiness and in 1899 became a 4–4–0 tender engine and was withdrawn in this state in 1934, the last of its class.
The train shed sheltering both platforms can be seen beyond the covered footbridge, while a water tank is near the leading engine.

20.5.1892 Author's collection

The rail being slewed inwards thus narrowing the gauge. In the middle distance can be seen Forder Viaduct
on the original line between Saltash and St Germans for which a diversion was subsequently constructed.

May 1892 Author's collection

The last broad gauge trains ran on 20 May and all broad gauge stock returned to Swindon for breaking up or conversion. Until it could be dealt with, this stock was stored on 15 miles of temporary sidings.

The last broad gauge train left Penzance at 9.45 p.m. on 20 May and, having ascertained from each stationmaster that all broad gauge stock had been despatched from his station and any adjacent branch line, a form was handed to the Civil Engineer's representative authorizing him to take possession of the line.

The actual work of conversion began at daybreak on 21 May. Much of the track was on longitudinal sleepers held to gauge by transoms and alternate transoms had already been prepared by being sawn to standard gauge length. The men's task was sawing through the other transoms, slewing a line of rails over and then repacking the ballast. By the evening of Saturday 21 May a standard gauge engine was able to run a trial trip from Exeter to Plymouth. There was still work to be completed on Sunday, especially in the larger station yards. Regular passenger trains operated on the standard gauge from 23 May, some coaches and engines of this gauge having been carried down previously on broad gauge wagons. Standard gauge goods stock was sent down on 23 May and goods services restarted on 24 May, the day the out-of-district workmen were returned home. Of the 196 broad gauge locomotives and 3,891 items of broad gauge rolling stock, 122 of the former and 1,879 of the latter were converted by July 1893.

At Digby & Sowton station opened on 23 May 1995, passengers board the 14.50 Exeter St David's to Exmouth worked by 150234. The cycle track on the far left is segregated from the foot path.

11.3.97 Author

The 1960s saw the closure of many stations in the West of England, but subsequent years saw others being opened, or re-opened. Sidmouth Junction, closed on 6 March 1967 re-opened as Feniton on 3 May 1971. This was followed by the re-opening of Pinhoe and Templecombe, while on the former GWR line stations were opened at new sites at Worle and Tiverton Parkway, and Ivybridge was re-opened. From May 1997 Okehampton station was served by trains on Sundays-only with a vintage bus service running through to Gunnislake.

In addition to booking ordinary tickets, railways in the West of England generated extra revenue by issuing cheap tickets to such events as markets, races and agricultural shows, while excursion tickets were offered to seaside and other holiday places. Some excursions were of a circular variety such as Bristol to Ilfracombe by paddle steamer and return by rail, or the rather more elaborate LSWR trip from London to Ilfracombe and Bideford by rail; then road coach to Clovelly, Bude and Camelford; to Wadebridge by rail; on to Newquay by coach and return to London via Wadebridge and the North Cornwall line. In the 1950s the West of England featured in quite a number of holiday expresses. For something like £2 10s 0d, on Monday to Friday a special train left a town, or an area, for a different holiday destination each day, passengers returning to their own beds each evening.

## FREIGHT YESTERDAY AND TODAY

Until the 1950s railways were the country's main carrier: coal, raw materials and finished products, farm and market-garden produce, fertilizers, goods for sale in shops, all travelled by rail and much of it carried to and from the railhead in railway vans and lorries. Some travelled in goods trains and maybe took several days to reach the destination, while parcels and some special traffic travelled by passenger or parcels train.

Coal was vitally important. It was used for domestic heating and cooking, industrial power and fuel for railway locomotives. Until the 1960s when central heating by either oil, electricity or gas became the norm, most stations in the West of England, except those in highly wooded areas, had a coal yard and at least one local merchant. To avoid paying demurrage charges, the coal was shovelled out of wagons into bunkers containing various grades and then as required shovelled into hundredweight sacks. In dry weather a few unscrupulous merchants wetted the coal 'to damp down the dust' and thus sold water for the price of coal. With the reduced demand for coal in the 1960s, smaller yards were closed and more economic coal concentration depots set up to serve a larger area. Most towns had their own gasworks, though increasing centralization gradually caused the closure of smaller works, while the introduction of North Sea gas in the early 1970s caused the demand for gas coal to cease. Some grades of coal used in the West of England came from the Bristol and Radstock field, while others came from South Wales or the Midlands.

Blandford Forum had a typical goods yard, part raised to rail level for the convenience of road vehicles. Tractor unit, registration VYT 816, is attached to a parcels van, while nearby is a flat-bed trailer. The articulated units were convenient in that they were flexible in confined spaces and a trailer could be loaded while the tractor was out on collection and delivery. Coal wagons stand in the furthest siding.

1965 C. Steane

The milk churn was a common sight at many stations, farmers bringing them to the platform. Their death knell was sounded on 1 October 1931 when the first GWR six-wheeled milk tank was filled at Lavington, Wiltshire. From then on, the trend was for local creameries to send lorries to collect churns from farms and then despatch the milk in rail tanks. The very first wholesale milk depot to be established in Britain opened at Semley, on the Salisbury to Exeter line, in 1871, and was designed primarily to serve the needs of London. In 1957 a total of 18 million gallons were despatched from milk depots at Semley, Sherborne, Chard Junction and Seaton Junction compared with 9 million gallons in 1939. Although no milk is carried by rail today, there is a possibility that it will be in the near future.

Market-garden traffic was very large. For instance, in 1945 new potato traffic from Cornwall and the Scillies called for 198 special trains carrying 39,707 tons, while in the same year the transportation of Cornish broccoli necessitated 466 special trains carrying 62,687 tons. In 1908 up to 300 wagons a day were dealt with at Weymouth Quay, and because of the short shelf-life of flowers, new potatoes and tomatoes from the Channel Islands, together with broccoli and other vegetables from France, rapid transport was essential. The last PERPOT (perishables and potatoes) train left Weymouth in 1970.

Cattle traffic was important to and from the many markets in the West of England. This gave station staff considerable work: cattle vans required disinfecting with white bleach after use and the pens had to be hosed down, sometimes using a water supply at very low pressure. To prevent the animals being uncomfortably rattled around a van, a

The interior of Blandford Forum goods shed showing the wide variety of goods carried by the railway: sacks, water heater, spades, crates, toilet pan. The goods office is in the far corner. It appears as if the platform height has been raised at some date.

1965 C. Steane

Class 8F 2–8–0 No. 48431 passes through Wilton North with a train to Salisbury. Behind the four box vans is a lengthy rake of coal wagons. No. 48431 was built at Swindon in 1944 for the LMS and loaned to the GWR. Twenty years later it is again working on GWR lines. It carries an 82F (Bath Green Park) shed plate. No. 48431 is preserved on the Keighley & Worth Valley Railway.

8.4.64 Author

Class 8F 2–8–0 No. 48706 shunting loaded coal wagons at Writhlington Colliery, Radstock. No. 48706, built at Brighton by the SR in 1944, was immediately put into LNER stock before eventually reaching the LMS in 1947.

c. January 1966 C. Steane

movable partition was provided and positioned according to the number of beasts the van contained, the exterior location being marked 'S' for small or 'M' for medium.

Until myxomatosis halted the trade in 1953–4, rabbits were despatched from Exmoor, Dartmoor and Cornwall. For several months each year, a train nicknamed 'The Rabbiter' started each evening from South Molton and picked up at most stations to Taunton. It consisted of two bogie parcels vans and occasionally a horsebox, in the absence of a more suitable vehicle. Suspended head-down and joined in pairs through the tendons of their hind legs, rabbits were packed in wooden crates. Newly trapped rabbits had a warm, musky and not unpleasant odour. Similarly the LSWR despatched baskets of rabbits from stations on the North Cornwall line and stations on the edge of Dartmoor, running through vans to Waterloo and Birmingham, those to the latter destination travelling via the Somerset & Dorset Joint Railway.

Messrs C. & T. Harris' sausage vans were familiar in the west of England. Pre-First World War Harris' outward traffic travelled in ordinary passenger brake vans, but in the postwar period special branded vehicles were used. The yellow roof boards were similar to those on the coaches of principal express trains, but were lettered: 'Harris Bacon & Wiltshire Sausages' and gave details of their workings such as Calne to Newcastle; Calne to Manchester; Calne to Paddington; Calne to Southampton & Portsmouth; and Calne to Cardiff. Messrs Harris' goods revenue account totalled £1,000 monthly, while on the passenger side, Calne outwards parcel revenue was, in the Bristol Division, second only to Bristol Temple Meads.

Old varieties of strawberries did not travel well and it was only with the introduction of Royal Sovereign at the turn of the century that consignments of this fruit could be

'2251' class 0–6–0 No. 2244 (82B St Philip's Marsh) heads a ballast train at Cheddar. The wagons on the left contain sleepers and chairs. Note the train shed covering the passenger station platforms in the distance and also the Mendip Hills in the background.

1.5.62 D. Holmes

'02' class 0–4–4T No. 30183 (72D Plymouth Friary) at its home shed. The compressed air equipment for motor train working can be seen on the smokebox and running plates.

13.5.56 the Revd Alan Newman

'N' class 2–6–0 No. 31837 ascends the gradient of 1 in 36 out of Ilfracombe.

August 1952 R.E. Toop

'West Country' class Pacific No. 34092 *City of Wells* passes St James' Park Halt with an Up ballast train from Meldon Quarry. Below the station nameboard appears a smaller plaque: 'For Exeter City Football Ground'. No. 34092 is preserved on the Keighley & Worth Valley Railway.

18.4.64 R.A. Lumber

'700' class 0–6–0 No. 30691 passes St James' Park Halt with an Up freight to Exmouth Junction. An Ivatt Class 2 2–6–2T heads a train, probably from Exmouth, away from the halt.

*c.* 1958 R.A. Lumber

An Up goods approaches Templecombe behind 'S15' class 4–6–0 No. 30830. No. 30830 is preserved on the Bluebell Railway.

30.6.50 Pursey Short

A Millfield School special headed by a 'Western' class diesel-hydraulic terminates at Castle Cary. The two GUVs provide accommodation for pupils' trunks. The flat-roofed signal-box opened on 27 October 1942 and replaced its predecessor, which had been destroyed by a bomb.

April 1976 W.E. Harbor/C.G. Maggs's collection

sent by rail. A large seasonal traffic grew up from four stations on the Cheddar Valley line and, at the height of the season, three strawberry specials were despatched in addition to the fruit carried on ordinary trains. Following the passage of vehicles containing this commodity, the strawberry smell lingered.

Before the season started, Yatton collected Fruit C and Siphon G vans, the Carriage & Wagon Department at Weston-super-Mare fixing boards 'Return Empty to Yatton'. After closure of the Cheddar Valley line in 1965, strawberries were brought by road to Yatton and up to a dozen vans were despatched on various trains. The growers did not always appreciate that trains had to keep to a timetable and imagined that their fruit could be simply loaded into a van while the train waited at the platform.

Fish traffic was important at some stations – particularly Brixham, St Ives and Penzance, the last two handling about 5,000 tons annually. The LSWR creamed off some of this traffic in 1871 when the West Cornwall Fishing Steamship Company began carrying large fish consignments to railheads at Bideford and Exmouth. In 1922 3,442 tons of fish left Padstow by rail.

Until the development of motorways, newspaper trains were important for carrying London morning papers to the west. A rather rarer sight was a bullion van, low-roofed, windowless and in GWR passenger coach livery, carrying gold to and from ships at Plymouth. Home removals were sometimes made by train, furniture being carried in a container, while farm removals required a whole train – passenger coach, furniture container on a flat truck, implements in wagons and livestock in cattle vans.

In 1963 Freight Concentration Depots were set up in the West of England and small goods yards were closed, traffic being 'collection and delivery' by road to and from the concentration depots. However, this system was not destined to be in use for long as the development of motorways, and supermarket chains operating their own transport, led to the closure of rail depots.

'County' class 4–6–0 No. 1024 *County of Pembroke* heads the Up 'North Mail' near Starcross. The Travelling Post Office was detached at Bristol Temple Meads.

24.3.51 Pursey Short

The Down 'Cornish Riviera Express' at Teignmouth behind No. 6025 *King Henry III* in blue livery. Behind the tender is a bullion van still painted in the GWR 'tea and cream' colour scheme.

21.9.48 Pursey Short

Today's freight traffic in the West of England is principally stone from Meldon, Whatley and Merehead; china clay at Fowey Harbour, Treviscoe & Kernick, and the proposed extension of the Bodmin & Wenford Railway to Poley's Bridge; LPG (liquid petroleum gas) from Furzebrook; oil and petrol tankers to various locations; nuclear flasks to and from Bridgwater; while a daily 'Bin Liner' train carries containers of rubbish from Bath and Bristol to a landfill site at Calvert, Buckinghamshire. At the time of writing, the possibilities of opening a rail-served freight village on the Salisbury line near Exeter airport are being explored.

'47XX' class 2–8–0 No. 4700 passes Powderham with an Up milk train.

23.7.49 Pursey Short

## PASSENGER TRAFFIC YESTERDAY AND TODAY

In the early days of railways many people had a very low standard of living, their income being at subsistence standard or below. For example, in 1845 a couple travelling from Bristol to Bath to seek employment only had sufficient cash for one of them to travel by rail, the other having to walk the distance of 12 miles.

Until early in the twentieth century the railway was really the only way to travel a distance exceeding that which could be walked or covered by a local horsebus or tram route. Businessmen, office workers, manual workers, schoolchildren, shoppers and commercial travellers with their samples, all used the train. After the Second World War the development of motor bus services and private cars resulted in a decline in season-ticket traffic in the West of England, but as roads become more and more congested and parking grows more difficult and expensive, rail travel has much to offer, Exmouth to Exeter being a prime example. Today the road journey to the city is slow and ends with difficulties in parking, whereas a relaxing and picturesque rail trip beside the Exe Estuary takes only 20 to 24 minutes. Long-distance rail travel can benefit the businessman: he can work en route, should he wish to, and arrive fresh, rather than jaded after driving himself. The opening of Parkway stations, and provision of good parking facilities at many stations, encourages rail use and can generate income from land formerly used as goods yards.

No. 6024 *King Edward I* at Stapleton Road, Bristol, heads 'The Kiddies' Express, Weston-super-Mare', which set off from Paddington and was routed via Badminton. It is seen here crossing from the Main to Relief line. No. 6024 is now preserved at the Didcot Railway Centre.

August bank holiday, *c.* 1939 E.J.M. Hayward

A Calne to Chippenham auto train arrives at Stanley Bridge Halt. The four vans behind the engine carry Messrs Harris' bacon products.

*c.* 1951 M.E.J. Deane

A GWR poster advertising the beauties of Cornwall.

1898 Author's collection

## RAILWAY DOCKS AND STEAMER SERVICES

Railway owned docks were important in the West of England, the most impressive being Millbay at Plymouth. The outer harbour was about 30 acres in extent and the inner basin 13 acres. The latter was used for the import and export of general goods, grain and so on, and over 200,000 sq ft of floor space was provided in the grain and transship sheds. Ocean liners stood offshore and GWR tenders shuttled between them and the docks providing a cheaper service than piloting and anchorage fees incurred at other ports. The number of liners using Plymouth more than doubled from 354 in 1921, when a total of 13,170 passengers landed, to 788 in 1929, when the annual passenger total exceeded 38,000.

To cater for and encourage this expanding traffic, from May 1929 the GWR commenced running Pullman cars in the Ocean Liner expresses. In 1931 the GWR substituted its own 'Super Saloons' for the Pullmans. These were more modern in style and, with an interior width of 9 ft, were the widest of all British main line coaches. They were named after members of the Royal family, and to ride in these luxurious vehicles a supplementary charge of 10s was paid in addition to the first-class fare.

4–6–0 No. 5021 *Whittington Castle* approaches Newton Abbot with an Up South American boat express after detaching a 'Flower' class 4–4–0 which had acted as pilot from Plymouth. 'Special Saloon' *Princess Mary* is third from the engine.

*c.* 1934 E.J.M. Hayward

In 1927 an electrically driven conveyor belt was installed at Millbay Docks to carry mail bags between ship tender and storage vans and it soon recouped its cost as operation only required a third of the manpower required by a human chain. By the mid-1950s the postwar development of air travel caused the number of liners using Plymouth to decrease to approximately 180 annually, while a further fall meant that the last Ocean Specials were run in 1962.

Bridgwater Docks had an area of 3½ acres and were important for transshipment between vessel and rail. The docks branch closed in April 1967. Fowey has 2,386 ft length of quayage with equipment for loading vessels with china clay brought by rail. Until closure in 1926 Newquay had 1,000 ft of quayage for vessels which arrived with coal and loaded away with china clay.

Although not railway owned, Weymouth was important for Channel Islands traffic, the GWR running services from 1889 and BR continuing to run trains from quay to London, latterly Waterloo, until 26 September 1987. As well as being used by passengers, the quay was also used during the season for transferring vast quantities of market-garden produce from ship to rail. The quay closed to goods in February 1971.

'1366' class 0–6–0PT No. 1368 waits to leave Weymouth Quay station with the Up 'Channel Islands Express' carrying passengers from the GWR steamer *St Helier*.

22.7.47 Pursey Short

'1P' class 0–4–4T No. 1397 (22A Bristol) shunts coal wagons at the S & DJR's Highbridge Wharf.

3.3.45 Pursey Short

The tide is out at the Weston, Clevedon & Portishead Light Railway's Wick St Lawrence Wharf on which stands a crane. Beyond is a pile driver. The bridge carrying the Weston to Clevedon line across the River Yeo can be seen in the left distance.

1921 E.H. Hazell

The GWR owned and worked the ferry between the railway at Kingswear and the trackless station at Dartmouth, SS *The Mew* carrying out this duty from 1908 till 1954.

In an attempt to siphon off some of the GWR's lucrative and prestigious ocean-liner traffic, in 1904 the LSWR built a station on Stonehouse Pool Improvement Company's land and in 1907 took over that concern. The LSWR owned a tender and visited the same vessels as those of the GWR. An agreement of 13 May 1910 ended competitive ocean-liner traffic from Plymouth to London and the LSWR service ceased on 28 May that year.

Between the First and Second World wars the port of Fremington, west of Barnstaple, was modernized by the SR and was second in importance only to Plymouth. Annually 50,000 tons of locomotive coal from South Wales was landed and distributed to SR sheds in the south-west. Cranes were provided for transferring clay from wagon to ship and in 1933 1,220 tons of clay bound for Spain were handled in four days. The quay closed on 30 March 1970.

For its size, the Somerset & Dorset Railway was remarkably active in the marine field. For a time it operated a passenger ferry from Burnham-on-Sea to Cardiff, while its cargo steamers were based at Highbridge and Bridgwater. Beyond Burnham station a 900-ft-long line ran down a pier where passengers could land at any state of the tide. As the gradient was too steep for locomotive operation, rolling stock was moved up and down by rope and capstan. From 1874 till 1932 the rails on the pier were used by the launching cradle of the lifeboat brought from its house on a siding. Highbridge Wharf handled timber from the Baltic ports, rails, coal and so on, while Caerphilly cheese made in Somerset was despatched to South Wales. For transshipping goods, the S&D provided steam cranes running on broad gauge track and dating from the time when the Somerset Central Railway used the 7 ft 0¼ in gauge. S&D shipping interests ceased in 1934, but until about 1950 the wharf was still used by other vessels. The S&D wharf on the River Parrett at Bridgwater closed in 1942.

The Weston, Clevedon & Portishead Light Railway built a wharf at Wick St Lawrence in about 1913, the company hoping to develop sea traffic to and from South Wales. The River Yeo being shallow, it was only suitable for use by ketches and sailing or motor barges. Traffic was light, a collier calling only every few months. Although the company advertised that 'Seaborne traffic can now be dealt with at Wick St Lawrence' on its timetables and buildings, the wharf was far from being a huge success.

## RAILWAY ARCHITECTURE

A wide variety of station architecture can be seen in the West of England, the finest being Bristol Temple Meads. It consists of Brunel's Tudor-style terminus matching many of the bridges and tunnels from Bath westwards, its impression of a gentleman's country seat boosting the confidence of nervous early passengers. Adjacent are the curved through platforms below Sir Matthew Digby Wyatt's splendid curved train shed. He was assisted by Francis Fox of the B&ER, the green and gold exterior canopy almost certainly being one of his designs as it is virtually identical to the one at Weston-super-Mare, which boasts another splendid station. On the right-hand side of Temple Meads

Gas-turbine locomotive No. 18000 at Temple Meads heads an express to Paddington. The curved roof of
Sir Matthew Digby Wyatt's train shed looms above the platform canopies of the 1930s' station extension.

*c.* 1954 M.E.J. Deane

station approach is F.C. Fripp's Jacobean-style B&ER office block. Yatton, formerly junction of the Cheddar Valley and Clevedon branches, is unusual in having two different types of Brunel building. The Down side has one in Tudor style with a flat, all-round awning, while that on the Up has an Italianate-style hipped roof. Bridgwater station has matching buildings with Georgian-style windows on both platforms.

As Taunton lay to the south of the line, Brunel's original station was built on the one-sided principle which he also adopted at Reading and Exeter. In order to avoid passengers crossing the line, and also to enable through trains to run clear of the platforms, he placed separate Up and Down stations on what was considered the Down track. Quite logically the Up station was at the London end of the layout. The two-storey former Down building, constructed in domestic style, is still extant.

Torquay has a delightful building of French-pavilion type with a cast-iron crest to its roof and dates from 1873. Both platforms have an attractive arcade with decorative canopy support columns now imaginatively painted to enhance their features.

Frome is the only working survivor of the many overall-roof timber stations built throughout the West of England. Chard Joint station, which closed in 1962, was unique in combining a Brunellian extended hipped roof Italianate brick building with a timber overall roof supported on an arcade of brick arches instead of the usual timber walls.

Crediton is another Brunel-style building and is curious for the fact that for many years it belonged to the rival LSWR. This was due to the station being built by the

'Castle' class 4–6–0 No. 5079 *Lysander* at Exeter St David's in charge of the Down 'Torbay Express'. The tall building, right, once supported an overall roof. Note 'British Railways' on the tender in Great Western lettering.

14.4.49 J.H. Bamsey

Staff outside the Bristol & Exeter booking office at Bridgwater station. A signalman, centre, wears a top hat; with him are three porters and a lad porter.

1859 P.J. Squibbs collection

Ex-LNER 'B1' class 4–6–0 No. 61251 *Oliver Bury* leaves Temple Meads for Plymouth on trial in the 1948 locomotive exchanges.

1948 Author's collection

The train shed at Penzance. 4–6–0 No. 4953 *Pitchford Hall* will take the 1.15 p.m. on the first leg of its journey to Paddington. No. 4953 is preserved on the Dean Forest Railway.

November 1937 E.J.M. Hayward

Exeter & Crediton Railway, a company which transferred from the B&ER to the LSWR camp. The buildings on both platforms are in Tudor style with flat all-round awnings. Torre station, another of Brunel's Italianate designs, is unusual because it is constructed of timber rather than stone or brick. St German's station, built in 1859 by Brunel for the Cornwall Railway, has a building on each platform, both with plain, flat awnings.

Several branch lines built by independent companies and later taken over by the GWR had stations designed by William Clarke. The first line on which his standard station appeared was the Bristol & North Somerset Railway which ran between Bristol and Radstock and opened in 1873. Neat functional buildings, they also appeared in the West of England on the Camerton branch, the Abbotsbury Railway, the Bridport Railway and the Kingsbridge & Salcombe Railway.

The introduction of the steam railmotor in the early years of the century gave rise to the building of unstaffed halts. These were often cheaply constructed of old sleepers with a corrugated-iron pagoda providing a simple shelter. The sleepers became dangerously slippery in wet weather, and in due course were replaced with a concrete surface.

The GWR owned two hotels in the West of England, taking over the Tregenna Castle at St Ives in 1878 and the Manor House Hotel, Moretonhampstead in 1930. From 1931,

'8750' class 0–6–0PT No. 9671 pauses at Chard Central with the 2.50 p.m. Taunton to Chard Junction. The station buildings are typical Brunellian.

5.4.58 E. Wilmshurst

'14XX' class 0–4–2T No. 1454 at Abbotsbury, the station building designed by William Clarke. The end
loading dock, lower left, looks as though it has not been used recently.

1947 J.H. Russell

for less wealthy patrons, four-, six- and eight-wheeled camp coaches were sited at many
of the picturesque stations in the West of England, their occupants being required to
arrive by rail and often voluntarily purchasing a weekly runabout ticket for the area.

Sir William Tite designed many of the LSWR stations. Salisbury was the last in his
Italianate style and has stone-trimmed round and square openings and a low-pitched roof
without a parapet. The glass-roofed platform, almost 800 ft in length, was the longest in
the country, all Up trains running through and then backing into the station on the
Down line. Owing to the close proximity of GWR premises, the position was so
cramped that when conditions became so intolerable that an Up platform needed to be
added, a separate station was built about a ¼ of a mile east of the original structure. The
connection through a narrow subway proved most inconvenient as Salisbury was
the junction of several routes and considerable numbers of passengers needed to change
trains. In 1901–2 the station was enlarged to four through roads with a bay at either end.
From 1932, when the GWR terminal passenger station closed, it also accommodated
that company's trains. Tite's station at Crewkerne included a steeply gabled three-storey
house adjoining a single-storey office building. Both are in the Tudor style and have
massive chimneys. Topsham station on the Exmouth branch is similar.

Camping Coach No. 13 at Tipton St John's.

26.9.49 J.H. Aston

The Midland Railway owned a splendid terminal station at Bath. The pseudo-Georgian block fronts on to the street and blends well with the city's architecture. Fortunately the building has been preserved and the slender Ionic columns can still be seen rising above the rusticated ground floor. A balustraded parapet conceals the roof line and excellently proportioned fenestration, well balanced by a delicate iron *porte-cochère*, which all complement the train shed beyond. This curved, all-over roof has a span of 66 ft and covers the platforms for a distance of 220 ft. An unusual feature was a bonded warehouse at the far end of one platform. This enabled rail vehicles containing wines and spirits consigned to local traders to be shunted into a secure building, where their contents could be lowered to the cellars extending the lengths of the station platforms, casks being carried on small narrow gauge wagons.

As a result of the hilly topography of the West of England its railways required many bridges and viaducts. A feature of Brunel's viaducts in Devon and Cornwall was that they were constructed of timber, the reason being that building was both quick and cheap – a great attraction to an impoverished company. The Cornwall Railway required no fewer than thirty-four viaducts on the 49 miles of main line between Saltash and Truro. The piers, generally of stone, were built at 66 ft centres. By keeping to standard dimensions, a stock of spare struts and beams could be maintained to fit any viaduct. The viaducts were designed so that any spar could be replaced without disturbing any other spar and that an exchange could be completed in an hour. Timber used in the viaduct was kyanized – soaked in a mercuric compound. This method of preservation was safer than creosoting, as

The timber trestle Keyham Viaduct under reconstruction and being adapted to support a metal span.
1899 Author's collection

BR Standard 'Britannia' class Pacific No. 70019 *Lightning* and '43XX' class 2–6–0 No. 6397 cross the Royal Albert Bridge with the Up 'Cornish Riviera Express'.

22.8.53 P.Q. Treloar

The retracting bridge over the River Parrett on the Bridgwater Docks branch. The portion shown slides left, and the section behind the photographer slides along to take its place.

8.10.66 Author

there was less danger of fire, although, as a precautionary measure, water tanks were placed at the ends of timber viaducts. Unfortunately none of these graceful viaducts remain, College Wood Viaduct on the Falmouth branch being, in 1934, the last to be replaced. In most instances the new stone viaducts were built alongside the old timber ones, so the original piers remain beside the new. Between Defiance Platform (Wearde signal-box) and St Germans a new double line replaced the old single line and avoided five timber viaducts.

The Royal Albert Bridge, built by Brunel in 1859 to carry the Cornwall Railway over the River Tamar at Saltash, is a splendid construction. It consists of two enormous wrought-iron curved tubes, 461 ft in length and supported on stone piers. From these tubes, hangers and chains support the rail track deck, and it is the only suspension bridge in the world to carry a railway.

Other less-notable, but interesting, GWR bridges included that immediately west of Bath station and the most oblique ever built of timber. Quay to quay the canalized river was 80 ft wide, but the bridge spanned 164 ft. On the Bristol Harbour branch was the unusual double-deck Ashton Swing Bridge with road above and rail beneath. At Highbridge, Brunel constructed Somerset Bridge to cross the River Parrett. This 100-ft span masonry arch had a rise of only 12 ft and was nearly twice as flat as his more famous bridge at Maidenhead, which his critics said was sure to fall. In truth, Brunel went rather too far. The foundations of Somerset Bridge shifted and although the arch was not damaged, Brunel would not move its supporting central timbers. These blocked the waterway and resulted in a protest being made. The foundations continued to settle, so Brunel used his ingenuity by substituting a timber-arch bridge using the same abutments.

At Bridgwater Docks was a rare telescopic bridge. Divided into three sections, steam operating machinery moved the first section sideways; then the main span across the river was drawn back into the vacated space. The third section remained fixed. The bridge was last moved in about 1953.

The LSWR built the impressive and slender Meldon Viaduct near Okehampton. Engineered by W.R. Galbraith and R.F. Church, it consists of six spans each of 85½ ft with a maximum height of 130 ft. The wrought-iron Warren girder spans are supported on wrought-iron lattice piers making it one of the very few all-metal viaducts in Britain. When the line was doubled a similar, but independent, viaduct was built alongside. It is on a 30 chains radius curve.

Calstock Viaduct on the Gunnislake branch is an impressive and picturesque structure, consisting of massive concrete blocks. There are said to be 11,148 in total, each weighing at least a ton. They were cast on site and finished to resemble stone. Built by Langs of Liskeard, the twelve arches each have a 60-ft span, the maximum rail height being 120 ft above the River Tamar. An interesting and unusual feature was that at its Cornish end was a wagon hoist with a vertical lift of 113 ft, one of the highest in the country. Traffic down to the quay below was principally bricks, but also some copper ore and granite; while upwards traffic was coal, timber and limestone. The volume of traffic declined and the hoist was dismantled in October 1934. The Gunnislake branch also crossed the 483-yd long Tavy Viaduct consisting of eight bow-strong girders, each spanning 111 ft 4 in, and nine masonry spans of 50 ft.

Chelfham Viaduct on the 1 ft 11½ in gauge Lynton & Barnstaple Railway has the honour of being the largest on a British narrow gauge railway. Built of yellow brick, it has eight 42-ft spans at a maximum 70 ft in height.

'43XX' class 2–6–0 No. 6344 crosses Castle Hill Viaduct, between Filleigh and South Molton with an Up train. The first three coaches bear a roof board 'Paddington and Ilfracombe'.

late 1920s A. Halls

## LOCOMOTIVES

With such a complicated subject as GWR locomotives, a general overview is difficult, but in the broad gauge era express passenger trains were hauled by single driving wheel engines of the 2–2–2 or 4–2–2 variety. The GWR's first goods engines were 2–4–0s, while those built subsequently had the 0–6–0 arrangement, the latter being the predominant broad gauge locomotive. The 0–6–0STs were also used for main line and branch goods work in addition to shunting. Sir Daniel Gooch's last locomotive design was the ugly and not very successful 'Metropolitan' class 2–4–0Ts, the first condensing tank engines in the country. All the GWR broad gauge engines were named but not numbered.

The B&ER had its own locomotive stock, and between 1849 and 1875 was independent of Swindon with its own locomotive works at Bristol. The B&ER locomotive superintendent James Pearson designed 2–2–2Ts for branch work and produced eight 4–2–4 well and back-tank engines for express duty. These unforgettable engines Nos 39–46 (the B&ER numbered their broad gauge engines) had enormous 9-ft diameter flangeless driving wheels. They were the fastest engines of their day and one achieved a speed of 81.8 mph down Wellington Bank. They were coke burners with a consumption of under 22 lb per mile. An unusual item was B&ER No. 29 *Fairfield*, a combined engine and coach designed and built by W.B. Adams in 1848. It worked on the Tiverton, Clevedon and Weston-super-Mare branches, but was sold in 1856. As the floor was within 9 in of the rails, passengers could board from ground level. Its coke consumption was 8.7 lb per mile.

The broad gauge 4–2–2 *Inkerman* driven by G. Eggar passes Worle Junction with the second part of the Down 'Flying Dutchman'. The signalman obeys the rule and displays a white flat as the road is clear. Note the mixed gauge track. Beyond the signal-box is the junction of the line from Weston-super-Mare.

1892 the Revd A.H. Malan

The South Devon Railway had to contend with fearsome gradients and, as existing GWR locomotive classes were not really suitable, Gooch designed two 4–4–0STs *Corsair* and *Brigand*. From 1 July 1851 the contractors Messrs Evans & Geach worked the line for ten years with 4–4–0ST and 0–6–0ST engines, the SDR taking over working on 1 July 1866. As on the GWR, the broad gauge locomotives only bore names until being added to the GWR's own stock on 1 February 1876. The SDR, which had its own locomotive works at Newton Abbot, supplied engines to the Cornwall Railway and the West Cornwall Railway.

With the approaching end of the broad gauge system, the GWR constructed convertible engines which were standard gauge locomotives fitted with broad gauge axles. In 1876 Armstrong built ten double-frame 0–6–0STs as convertibles with wheels outside the frames and twenty of his 'Standard Goods' 0–6–0s were converted to broad gauge. Fitted with old broad gauge tenders, these looked most odd behind the standard gauge width cabs. Other convertibles were 2–4–0Ts, of which five became tender

'Star' class 4–6–0 No. 4056 *Princess Margaret* at Bristol, Temple Meads with a Down parcels train.
1951 W.H. Harbor/C.G. Maggs's collection

'28XX' class 2–8–0 No. 3845 about to enter Whiteball Tunnel with '5101' class 2–6–2T No. 4136 assisting at the rear. No. 3845 is preserved.

22.4.51 Pursey Short

4–6–0 No. 1011 *County of Chester* in black livery leaves Bristol Temple Meads with an express. Ex-LMS 'Compound' 4–4–0 No. 41064 is on the right.

1951 W.H. Harbor/C.G. Maggs's collection

4–6–0 No. 6900 *Abney Hall* outside Bristol, Bath Road, shed. The substantial coaling stage surmounted by a water tank is on the right; the repair shop is on the left.

1951 W.H. Harbor/C.G. Maggs's collection

4–6–0 No. 6851 *Hurst Grange* with small tender stands on the Weymouth shed turntable. The engine is in black livery, with a red ground to name and number plates.

27.8.50 Pursey Short

BR Standard 'Britannia' class Pacific No. 70024 *Vulcan* arriving at Exeter St David's with the 11.00 a.m. Paddington to Plymouth. An SR 'E1/R' class engine waits in the banker siding, left.

25.4.52 T. Reardon

engines for working such trains as the 'Cornishman'. The 0–4–2ST convertibles were so unsteady that the last was constructed as an 0–4–4T with short side and back tanks instead of a saddle tank. To a certain extent this modification proved successful and the others of the class were similarly modified, but between 1899 and 1902 the class was rebuilt as 4–4–0 tender engines.

In 1903 the GWR purchased a four-cylinder compound 4–4–2 designed by de Glehn, chief mechanical engineer of the Northern Railway of France. Named *La France*, it worked the 'Cornish Riviera Express' and other trains. Churchward was able to use some of its features to develop his 'simple' 4–6–0s and make them just as economical without the additional expense of a compound engine.

Practically all types of GWR standard gauge engines worked in the West of England including, between 1905 and the 1930s, steam railmotors, which were a combined passenger coach and locomotive. When these generated more traffic than they could handle, auto-fitted engines were used which could have up to two auto coaches at each

Grubby looking BR Standard Class 9F 2–10–0 No. 92238 (82E Bristol Barrow Road) at Yatton.

2.2.65 M. Wathen

A line-up of 4–6–0s at Penzance shed: No. 1011 *County of Chester*; No. 6855 *Saighton Grange* and an
unidentified 'County'. A 'devil', used to prevent freezing, can be seen below the water crane.

*c.* 1959 P.Q. Treloar

BR Standard Class 5MT 4–6–0 No. 73001 (82E Bristol Barrow Road) approaches Bradford-on-Avon with a summer special.

29.8.64 the Revd Alan Newman

Inside Westbury shed: No. 4993 *Dalton Hall* and No. 6874 *Haughton Grange*. The smoke troughs assist in keeping the shed smoke-free.

12.8.64 the Revd Alan Newman

Ex-LMS 'Coronation' class Pacific No. 46236 *City of Bradford* at Westbury with the 8.30 a.m. Plymouth to Paddington express during the 1948 Locomotive Exchanges.

19.5.48 Pursey Short

Oil-burning No. 3950 *Garth Hall* has just relieved an SR loco at Salisbury on the 10.35 a.m. Portsmouth Harbour to Cardiff train.

13.3.48 Pursey Short

end. Right up to dieselization a Pannier tank engine sandwiched between four coaches was a common sight in the Plymouth area.

Due to weight restrictions across the Royal Albert Bridge over the River Tamar, no 'Kings' or '47XX' class 2–8–0s could be seen in Cornwall. '43XX' class 2–6–0s were the largest engines handling traffic on the Norton Fitzwarren to Barnstaple line, their steps cut to a width of 8 ft 4 in to allow sufficient clearance when working over the SR's line to Ilfracombe. Also working expresses over this line were '45XX' class 2–6–2Ts. To speed working over single lines, in the 1930s automatic tablet exchange apparatus was fitted to some engines working the Barnstaple and Minehead branches.

The '44XX' class 2–6–2Ts were nearly all confined to the West of England. Similar to the '45XX' class, but with 4 ft 1½ in driving wheels instead of 4 ft 7½ in, they were particularly suited to the Princetown branch abounding in steep gradients combined with severe curves.

The Weymouth Quay tramway, running mostly through streets for a mile to the Channel Islands steamers, used particularly interesting engines. The first was a South Devon 2–4–0T followed by two B&ER 0–6–0Ts built for the Culm Valley Light Railway in Devon; No. 1391 *Fox*, a West Cornwall Railway 0–4–0ST; No. 1337 *Hook Norton*, originally owned by the Hook Norton Ironstone Partnership; two 0–6–0STs from the Whitland & Cardigan Bay Railway. LNWR 0–4–0ST No. 3033 appeared in 1917 to assist with wartime traffic. Then there were No. 2194 *Kidwelly* and No. 2195 *Cwm Mawr*, ex-Burry Port & Gwendraeth Valley Railway 0–6–0STs; and an engine of the same wheel arrangement ex-Alexandra Docks & Railway, while yet another was ex-Cornwall Minerals Railway. In fact the first Standard GWR engine allocated to the tramway was a '1366' class 0–6–0PT in 1935. The final steam engines were the much larger Ivatt Class 2 2–6–2Ts.

Ex-War Department 2–8–0 No. 79235 passes Teignmouth station with an Up goods.

21.9.48 Pursey Short

Shed scene at Plymouth Laira, right to left: '43XX' class 2–6–0 No. 6319; '45XX' class 2–6–2T No. 4590; '94XX' class 0–6–0PTs No. 8426 and No. 9433; '57XX' class 0–6–0PT No. 8709. The ash pit is on the left.

13.5.56 the Revd Alan Newman

Lines in Plymouth Docks had tight curves necessitating engines with a very short wheelbase. In 1910 Churchward designed the '1361' class 0–6–0STs which were a modernized version of the Cornwall Minerals Railway 0–6–0STs dating back to 1873. The CMR engines were unusual in that they were specially designed to work in pairs back-to-back.

From the 1930s onwards, as workers were granted an annual holiday, summer Saturdays became very busy as resorts in the West of England became popular. On these days traffic was so heavy that seat regulation had to be obtained to ensure that trains were not overcrowded. Mixed traffic engines proved most useful as from Mondays to Fridays they could haul goods trains and on Saturdays work the extra passenger trains. Providing coaching stock for these trains was uneconomic as the vehicles could only be utilized for a few summer Saturdays and stood idle for perhaps 360 days of the year. This holiday traffic produced a very variable traffic pattern. On Mondays to Fridays passenger trains from Paddington to the West averaged less than one an hour, but on summer Saturdays increased to as many as eight.

During the Second World War USA-built 2–8–0s, War Department Austerity 2–8–0s and Swindon-built LMS Class 8F 2–8–0s appeared on the GWR.

In view of the switchback gradients of the line between Salisbury and Exeter, the locomotive depots at these points and at Yeovil were given an allocation of the more powerful mixed traffic classes – 'S15' 4–6–0s and 'N' and 'U' class 2–6–0s suitable for intermediate passenger and freight traffic to replace older 4–4–0 and 0–6–0 classes.

Plymouth Laira shed: '8750' class 0–6–0PT No. 3629; 4–6–0 No. 7820 *Dinmore Manor*; '94XX' class
0–6–0PT No. 9467 and high on the coal stage road '8750' class No. 3686.

13.5.56 the Revd Alan Newman

When the Barnstaple to Ilfracombe line was approaching completion the LSWR
consulted Beyer, Peacock & Co. regarding suitable locomotives to work the 1 in 36
gradients and was recommended a light 0–6–0 similar to those purchased and found
completely satisfactory by the Swedish Government Railway. Initially three were ordered
and became known as 'Ilfracombe Goods' – though in practice they also worked
passenger trains.

Adams designed the 'B4' class 0–4–0Ts for working the sharply curved Cattewater and
Sutton Harbour lines at Plymouth. The class also worked goods trains on the Turnchapel
branch, spark-arresting chimneys enabling them to safely shunt the timber yard at
Oreston. The Turnchapel and Exmouth branches also saw the LSWR steam railmotors.

The broad gauge North Devon Railway, leased by the contractor Thomas Brassey,
used interesting engines. Most of the stock was obtained second hand from the Midland
Railway. Built by Stothert, Slaughter & Co., of Bristol which held a contract for working
the broad gauge Bristol to Gloucester line, they were sold to the MR in 1845 and
became surplus to requirements when the Midland converted the line to standard gauge
in 1854. Brassey's contract for working the North Devon terminated on 1 August 1862
and the broad gauge engines and rolling stock were taken over by the LSWR. The final

'West Country' class Pacific No. 34013 *Okehampton*, hauling a Down goods on WR metals, encounters a Weymouth-bound DMU at Westbury.

26.2.66 the Revd Alan Newman

Class 8F 2–8–0 No. 48669 (2E Northampton) built by the SR at Brighton in 1944 for the LMS, hauls a Down freight over WR metals to Bradford-on-Avon.

15.8.64 the Revd Alan Newman

'Merchant Navy' class Pacific No. 35021 *New Zealand Line* at Weymouth shed.

30.8.53 the Revd Alan Newman

'King Arthur' class 4–6–0 No. 30743 *Lyonesse* with a Weymouth to Bournemouth train has passed over the curve in the lower right-hand corner and reversed its train into the terminal Up platform at Dorchester South. To avoid such a reversal, a platform on the through Up line was opened 28 June 1970. Bridge plate No. 121, just in front of the engine, marks the subway to the Down platform.

20.9.52 A.E. West

'0415' class 4–4–2T No. 30583 (72A Exmouth Junction) runs round coach Set No. 44 at Lyme Regis.
Prominent are buffer stops constructed from old rails. No. 30583 is preserved on the Bluebell Railway.

*c.* 1955 Author's collection

'0415' class 4–4–2Ts No. 30583 and No. 30584 at Combpyne with an Up train. Sleepers are being replaced.
A camping coach stands centre left.

*c.* 1955 Author's collection

LSWR broad gauge daily goods ran on 30 April 1877 but Exeter to Crediton continued to be used by GWR broad gauge freight trains until May 1892.

The Plymouth, Devonport & South Western Junction Railway had its own locomotive stud – one 0–6–0T and two 0–6–2Ts, all three named as well as numbered. For working the North Devon & Cornwall Junction Light Railway which opened in 1925 between Torrington and Halwill Junction, the SR used tender engines. In the event, turning proved difficult and since working 20½ miles tender-first proved unpleasant, an alternative class of locomotive was sought. In 1927 and 1928 ex-London, Brighton & South Coast Railway 'E1' class 0–6–0Ts were rebuilt into 0–6–2Ts using spare trailing axles. At the same time their bunkers were enlarged and the engines re-classified as 'E1R'. They were also utilized for banking duties from Exeter St David's to Central. From 1940 to 1942 the lines from Barnstaple to Bideford and to Braunton were patrolled by an armoured train which was intended to repel a German invasion. Motive power was ex-LNER 'F4' class 2–4–2T No. 7077, also suitably armoured.

From 1950 Bulleid Pacifics worked through from Waterloo to Exeter. The track was so splendid that there was practically no restriction to the downhill speeds and in the 1950s and '60s Down trains frequently achieved speeds of 80 mph plus at Gillingham, Sherborne, Axminster, Honiton and Broad Clyst – in fact the SR's speed record of 104 mph was achieved at Axminster by a rebuilt 'Merchant Navy' Pacific.

'Merchant Navy' and the 4–6–0 classes were prohibited from working west of Exeter due to load limitation on bridges. The light-weight 'West Country' class Pacifics were an

Ex-LMS Ivatt Class 2MT No. 41283 at Yeovil Town shed.

2.4.65 the Revd Alan Newman

A contrast in locomotive size at Yeovil Junction: left, 'M7' class 0–4–4T No. 30046 leaves for Yeovil Town and right is 'Merchant Navy' class Pacific No. 35013 *Blue Funnel*.

30.10.54 the Revd Alan Newman

Near Tisbury 'S15' class 4–6–0 No. 30842 heads the 12.16 p.m. Templecombe to Bournemouth West via Salisbury.

4.8.62 Author

'T9' class 4–4–0 No. 30717 (72A Exmouth Junction) at Wadebridge shed. It carries Exeter Central to Padstow route discs.

14.5.51 J.H. Bamsey

'0415' class 4–4–2T No. 30583 at Seaton Junction, having shunted the through Seaton to Waterloo coach on to the Up train, waits the passing on the through road of an Up express hauled by 'Merchant Navy' class Pacific No. 35009 *Shaw Savill* before re-crossing all tracks back to the Seaton branch on the extreme left.

16.9.50 S.W. Baker

A ballast train from Meldon Quarry leaving Exeter St David's for Exeter Central headed by Ivatt Class 2MT 2–6–2T No. 41307 and 'N' class 2–6–0 No. 31842 and banked in the rear by ex-London, Brighton & South Coast Railway 'E1/R' class 0–6–2Ts No. 32135 and No. 32124.

10.5.56 R.T. Coxon

Triple-headed Down passenger train at Exeter St David's: 'T9' class 4–4–0 No. 30727; 'West Country' class Pacific No. 34035 *Shaftesbury* and 'N' class 2–6–0 No. 31845.

24.7.54 J.H. Bamsey

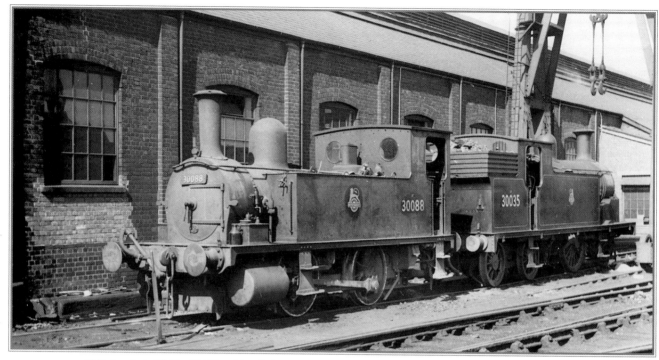

'B4' class 0–4–0T No. 30088 and 'M7' class 0–4–4T No. 30035 stand near a crane at Plymouth Friary shed.

13.5.56 the Revd Alan Newman

important addition to the Exeter to Plymouth and Ilfracombe routes where the working of passenger trains over steep gradients had been in the hands of 2–6–0 or 4–4–0 engines. The 'West Country' engines were not the complete answer, for one observer watched the 'Atlantic Coast Express' with a Pacific front and rear leave Ilfracombe with much slipping, while a GWR 2–6–0 with a similar load departed without any loss of adhesion and its acceleration was such that the SR 'N' class 2–6–0 assisting was left behind, only to catch up on the 1 in 36 gradient beyond the station.

The broad gauge Somerset Central Railway was worked by B&ER locomotives and the standard gauge Dorset Central Railway by those of the LSWR. When the SCR and DCR amalgamated to set up the Somerset & Dorset Railway it created its own stud of engines, principally George England 2–4–0s, John Fowler 0–6–0s and Fox, Walker 0–6–0STs. They were maintained at Highbridge Works. When the S&DR was taken over in 1875 by the LSWR and MR to become the Somerset & Dorset Joint Railway, modified Midland types were used, though from 1886 painted in the joint company's blue livery. These engines were 4–4–0 and 0–4–4Ts for passenger duty and 0–6–0s for freight. In 1906 the need was felt for a more powerful goods engine, but the weight of such a machine proved a problem. No suitable MR class was available, so a special one was designed. The first 2–8–0 emerged from Derby Works in 1914 and the class proved most successful at hauling goods trains over the Mendip Hills and by 1925 their numbers totalled eleven. In 1922 five MR-type Class 4 0–6–0s joined the S&DJR stock and proved equally happy on goods and express passenger services.

'E1/R' class 0–6–2T No. 32697 banking the 11.00 a.m. Plymouth to Brighton up the gradient of 1 in 37 at Exeter between St David's and Central stations.

30.7.59 R.A. Lumber

'M7' class 0–4–4T No. 30021 entering Salisbury station with empty coaching stock. The GWR-built Salisbury 'C' signal-box stands on the right.

18.10.62 the Revd Alan Newman

On the left re-built 'West Country' class Pacific No. 34101 *Hartland* is about to come off a Portsmouth Harbour to Cardiff train at Salisbury. Un-rebuilt 'West Country' No. 34106 *Lydford* is on the right.

18.10.62 the Revd Alan Newman

'S15' class 4–6–0 No. 30841 at Salisbury loco depot. No. 30841 is preserved on the North Yorkshire Moors Railway.

23.4.53 the Revd Alan Newman

'N' class 2–6–0 No. 31859 at Launceston with a Waterloo to Padstow train. The signal-box is unusual in having two frames: one for the GWR lines beyond the box and another for those of the SR.

11.7.64 R.A. Lumber

'A12' class 2–4–0WT No. 30587 at Wadebridge. No. 30587 is preserved on the South Devon Railway.

14.5.51 J.H. Bamsey

'02' class 0–4–4T No. 30203 at Padstow. Its train is in carmine and cream livery, but the coach of Set
No. 180 is green.

August 1954 P.Q. Treloar

Rebuilt 'West Country' class Pacific No. 34028 *Eddystone* at Wool with a Weymouth to Bournemouth train.
No. 34028 is preserved.

*c.* 1954 Dr T.R.N. Edwards

'T9' class 4–4–0 No. 30716 outside Yeovil Town shed in the new BR Standard livery of black lined cream, red and grey.

30.4.49 Pursey Short

BR Standard Class 4MT 2–6–0 No. 76013 drifts through Bournemouth Central with a Down goods.

13.6.64 the Revd Alan Newman

The Weston, Clevedon & Portishead Light Railway owned a relatively large and varied locomotive stock for a rural line only 14¼ miles in length. No fewer than sixteen engines worked the line at one time or another and most were bought second, or even third hand. When the WC & PLR opened in 1898 two of the engines were 2–2–2WTs. At various times the company owned several 2–4–0Ts, but the commonest type consisted of 0–6–0 tank engines. These varied from the contractor's saddle tank variety to ex-LBSCR 'Terrier' side tanks.

The WC&PLR was an early user of internal-combustion engines, in 1921 purchasing a Drewery Car Co. four-wheeled petrol-engined railcar seating thirty passengers and with running and maintenance costs at a mere sixpence a mile. During busy periods it could haul a trailer seating twenty-four, or a wagon for milk churns or luggage which would not fit readily on the roof of the railcar, spare cans of petrol, often with missing caps, were carried inside the railcar and as smoking was allowed it was most fortunate that no accident occurred. In 1934 a larger Drewry railcar was bought from the SR. It seated twenty-six passengers and had a separate compartment for churns and luggage. Pleased with the 1921 railcar's success, the WC&PLR purchased a Fordson tractor fitted with railway wheels and used it as a shunter on the Wick St Lawrence Wharf branch. While being towed from Wick to Clevedon at the rear of a train, it jumped the rails and was damaged beyond repair before the train could be halted. It was replaced with an improved model.

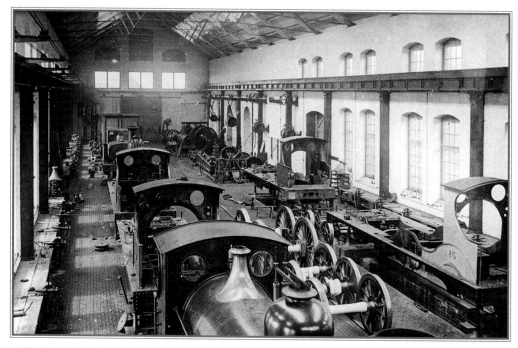

The Somerset & Dorset Joint Railway's locomotive erecting and fitting shop at Highbridge. The cab and frames of 4–4–0 No. 15 are to the right.

*c.* 1894 Author's collection

Vertical boiler Sentinel four-wheeler No. 47191 for use under the low 'Marble Arch'. It is coupled to an ash wagon. Radstock loco shed is on the left.

14.8.59 Author

Class 2P 4–4–0 No. 40564 and Class 5 4–6–0 No. 44826 climb the gradient of 1 in 50 through Lyncombe Vale, Bath, with a Birmingham to Bournemouth West train.

June 1949 Author

The ramshackle-looking Bath loco depot: Class 4F 0–6–0 No. 44523, left, and S&D Class 7F 2–8–0 No. 13805 below the ash gantry.

15.8.49 Author

Class 3F 0–6–0T No. 47465 at the Radstock start of the 8-mile-long push to Masbury Summit. S&D Class 7F 2–8–0 No. 53807 is at the front of the midday freight.

9.11.54 the Revd Alan Newman

Class 1P 0–4–4T No. 58072 (71J Highbridge) fitted with condensing apparatus for use in London tunnels, works the 6.05 p.m. Bath Green Park to Binegar. At one time this class worked through passenger trains between Bath and Bournemouth.

25.4.55 the Revd Alan Newman

Ex-S&D Class 3F 0–6–0 No. 43201 (71J Highbridge) on the middle road at Evercreech Junction with a train to Highbridge.

26.4.54 the Revd Alan Newman

Class 1P 0–4–4T No. 58086 at Highbridge shed which closed on 11 May 1959. Notice the fire-iron stand.

29.8.56 Author

Class 2P 4–4–0 No. 40505 heads a Bournemouth West to Templecombe stopping train at Shillingstone. Whitaker's tablet catcher can be seen protruding near the front of the tender.

9.9.50 Pursey Short

Class 5 4–6–0 No. 44830 (22C Bath Green Park) in charge of the 'Pines Express' approaching Templecombe Junction.

30.6.50 Pursey Short

Class 1P 0–4–4T No. 58088 approaching Templecombe with the 2.05 p.m. Burnham-on-Sea to Templecombe.

30.6.50 Pursey Short

Class 4F 0–6–0 No. 44102 leaves Midford with the 3.20 p.m. Bath Green Park to Templecombe. The hut contains a ground frame giving access to the Up goods siding.

14.8.56 Author

Ex-S&D Class 4F 0–6–0 No. 44559 and SR 'West Country' Pacific No. 34044 *Woolacombe* leave Bath with a Bath to Bournemouth West train. Note the hand crane to the left.

30.7.55 the Revd Alan Newman

BR Standard Class 9F 2–10–0 No. 92220 *Evening Star* leaves Bournemouth West with a train to Bristol.
No. 92220 is preserved by the National Railway Museum.

30.9.63 the Revd Alan Newman

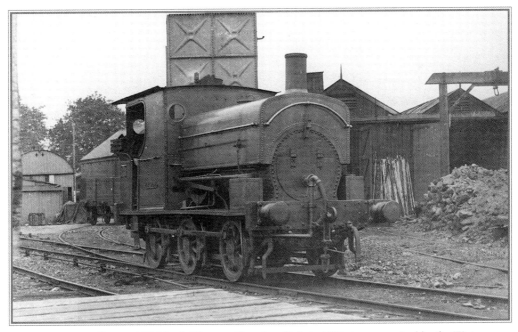

Manning Wardle 0–6–0ST No. 3 *Weston* at Clevedon. Built in 1881, it was acquired by the Weston,
Clevedon & Portishead Railway in 1906 and withdrawn in 1940.

*c.* 1932 Author's collection

Ex-GWR 2–4–0T No. 1384 on the WC&PLR at Portishead; latterly it was named *Hesperus*. The GWR acquired it from the Watlington & Princes Risborough Railway.

1909 Author's collection

Ex-SR Drewry petrol-engined railcar on the WC&PLR at Weston-super-Mare. Built in 1928, it seated twenty-six passengers. A milk stage can be seen right of the signal – one of the few signals on this light railway.

1937 Author's collection

## MAIN LINE INTERNAL COMBUSTION ENGINED POWER

In the 1930s, Simplex petrol-engined shunting locomotives were used at Taunton concrete works and Bridgwater Docks. In 1936 diesel railcar No. 10, constructed by AEC at Southall, commenced a service between Bristol and Weymouth, subsequently this being worked by twin units Nos 35 and 36, or 37 and 38. In addition to this service, most of the branches in the Bristol area saw a diesel railcar. In 1946 the GWR ordered a gas turbine locomotive from the Swiss firm of Brown-Boveri, but it was not delivered until 1950 when BR numbered it 18000. The Metropolitan-Vickers Electrical Co. Ltd built a gas turbine locomotive which was numbered 18100. Both machines were found to use almost as much fuel when idling, or running under reduced power, and had no advantage over diesel-electric locomotives. No. 18100 was withdrawn in 1958 and No. 18000 followed in 1960.

As Devon and Cornwall were some distance from the South Wales steam coal collieries, it made sense to convert the West of England to diesel haulage at an early date. The WR expressed individuality by favouring diesel-hydraulic, rather than diesel-electric traction. The 'Warship' class appeared in 1958 and the 'Western' class three years later, signalling the demise of 'Kings', 'Castles' and '47XX' 2–8–0s; while diesel-hydraulic 'Hymeks' introduced in 1961 replaced 'Halls' and other mixed traffic 4–6–0s. Meanwhile various types of DMU replaced passenger trains hauled by tank engines. Most of the

Diesel railcars No. 35 and No. 36, with intermediate trailer, working the 8.05 a.m. Bristol Temple Meads to Weymouth. To gain income from investment the viaduct was built as cottages, but due to damp and vibration were never used as such. Twerton Tunnel Down distant signal, no less than 1,000 yds from the box, is at the rear of the train.

20.4.54 Author

Metropolitan-Vickers 2,450 hp gas-turbine No. 18100 at Exeter St David's with the Down 'Cornish Riviera Express'. Built in 1951, it was withdrawn in 1958 and converted by its makers into a 25Kv electric locomotive used for LMR main line electric crew training.

1952 N. Wellings

'Warship' class diesel-hydraulic D831 *Monarch* shunts milk tanks at Yeovil Junction.

15.4.67 Author

Hymek diesel-hydraulic D7039 and No. 6907 *Davenham Hall* west of Bath with the 4.25 p.m. Cardiff to
Portsmouth Harbour. Diesel locomotives were usually coupled in front, rather than behind a steam engine,
in order to avoid their ventilating fans sucking dirt into the machinery.

22.6.63 Author

locomotive depots in the West of England had ousted steam by mid-1964 and in May of
that year steam working was banned on the WR west of Bridgwater and Castle Cary.
The last of the diesel-hydraulics were withdrawn in 1977 having been replaced by classes
brought in from other regions such as the Class 50s, the first on the WR to be officially
capable of 100 mph. Apart from the Somerset & Dorset which never had diesel haulage,
steam was eradicated from the WR by the end of 1965.

In 1976 an HST service from Paddington to Bristol was introduced, making it second
in the world in terms of speed and frequency. By the end of that decade HSTs reached
Plymouth and Penzance, then, with HSTs being responsible for services from the West of
England to the North and Scotland, locomotive passenger haulage was almost a thing of the past.

SR diesel-electric locomotives Nos 10201/2/3 appeared on Waterloo to Weymouth and
Exeter trains in the early 1950s and from 1953 ex-LMS diesel-electric Nos 10000/1 shared
these duties, the Railway Executive believing it best that they be maintained alongside SR
diesels rather than in dirty London Midland Region steam sheds. All five diesel-electrics were
transferred to the LMR in 1955, but steam remained king on the Salisbury to Exeter line
until 1964 when WR diesel-hydraulic 'Warships' began taking over duties, though some
steam still survived until 1965. In 1980, the Class 50s which had been displaced from the
Paddington route by HSTs took over the Waterloo to Exeter line from the Class 33s which
had usurped the 'Warships'. Locomotive working ended on 10 July 1993 when Class 159
units (3-car sets) specially constructed for the Waterloo–Salisbury–Exeter service took over.

To enable through trains to continue to run to Weymouth after the Bournemouth
electrification in 1967, a Class 33 hauled a 4-TC trailer set which had formed the front
of a Waterloo to Bournemouth EMU set, and then pushed it from Weymouth back to
Bournemouth where it was coupled to the rear of an EMU to Waterloo. The Weymouth
line was electrified in May 1988. Incidentally, when Weymouth shed closed in July 1967,
it was the last ex-GWR shed to be closed to main line steam.

AC Cars four-wheel railbus W79975 at Yeovil Town. It worked the shuttle service to Yeovil Junction.

2.4.65 the Revd Alan Newman

2,000 hp diesel-electric No. 10203 passing Seaton Junction with the 4.30 p.m. Exeter Central to Waterloo.

14.6.54 S.W. Baker

Diesel-electric No. 33115 at Weymouth ready to push the 17.34 on the Weymouth to Bournemouth leg of its trip to Waterloo.

4.8.81 Author

Class 421 four-car electric Set 1244 leaving Upwey with the 11.53 Weymouth to Bournemouth.

14.6.88 Author

## CONCRETE DEPOTS

Sited at the east end of Taunton station was the GWR concrete depot. Throughout the years it provided such items as fence and loading gauge posts, paving slabs, signal-box coal bins and, during the Second World War, 'pot'-type concrete sleepers for use in sidings, goods loops and branch lines, in order to conserve timber sleepers for main lines where speeds were higher. In its later years the depot produced full-length concrete sleepers and bridge sections, the former being cast around rods in tension. From 1963 the depot took over work hitherto carried out by the SR's Exmouth Junction depot, but later the Taunton depot itself succumbed to closure in 1995.

The concrete works at Exmouth Junction was started in 1913 by the LSWR's chief engineer, J.W. Jacomb-Hood, for manufacturing an extremely wide range of articles: concrete post and rail fencing, panel fencing, cable boxes, wicket gates, mile and gradient posts, Meyrick Patent concrete sleeper blocks, station name boards, lamp posts, loading gauge posts, signal wire pulley stakes, saddles for signal rods, trunking for point rodding, crank frames, steps and stringers and platform walls – that is the part of the platform between the track ballast and platform edging.

The works site measured 175 ft by 1,000 ft and advantage was taken of the ground's natural slope by having all incoming material, such as stone chippings, sand, cement and steel for reinforcement delivered at a higher level, the lower siding used for the departure of finished products. Aberthaw was the main supplier of cement while stone chippings came from the LSWR's Meldon Quarry and sand from the Taw and Torridge estuary raised by dredger and carried by barge to Fremington where it was loaded into wagons. Mixed concrete was distributed to various areas of the yard by means of hand-pushed trolleys running on 2 ft gauge track.

William Holt Shortt, Divisional Engineer, was an imaginative man and from 1928 onwards the works expanded. Shortt designed concrete footbridges, and additional items manufactured from concrete were sectional buildings, cables, signal and telephone posts, yard lighting poles and, during the Second World War, air-raid shelters. Before 1939 there were 140 employees and this number expanded to a maximum of 186 in the postwar era.

---

**Material Trains to and from the Engineer's Yard**

An engine with vehicles attached may work between the Goods Yard and the Engineer's Yard without a brake van in the rear. The Shunter must ride in, or walk alongside, the last vehicle, the hand-brake of which must be effectively applied.

During clear weather, vehicles may be propelled as between East Junction and East Loop on the Up Loop Line.

This working is only permitted with the engine at the Creech Junction end, and a tail lamp must be placed on the last vehicle.

The Signalmen concerned must inform each other on the telephone of the movement to be made.

---

Instructions for working material trains to and from the Engineer's Yard, Taunton, from the *Sectional Appendix to the Working Timetable and Books of Rules and Regulations, Exeter Traffic District*, 1960.

Wagons in the BR concrete yard at Taunton. It closed in 1995.

1.8.79 Author

## RAILWAY BUSES

In the last century, railways either ran, or supported, a certain number of road coach routes. For example in 1874 the B&ER ran a daily coach from Barnstaple to Ilfracombe and in 1890 the GWR agreed to pay the proprietors of the Dulverton to Minehead coach a subsidy of 10s per trip during the months of July, August and September. However, it was not until early in the twentieth century that railway bus services really developed; in fact it was Sir George Newnes, chairman of the narrow gauge Lynton & Barnstaple Railway, who introduced the first railway motor bus feeder service in Britain. Two Milnes-Daimler twenty-two-seater motor wagonettes inaugurated the Blackmoor station to Ilfracombe service on 30 May 1903. Following difficulties with the police when vehicles were found 'speeding above 8 mph', the buses were sold to the GWR which used them to start a Helston to Lizard service on 17 August 1903, a rather cheaper expedient than building a proposed light railway. On 31 October 1903 the GWR introduced a service linking Newlyn, Penzance and Marazion.

Services were extended to cover much of Cornwall, South Devon, the area between Bridgwater and Portishead, around Frome and Trowbridge and in the Weymouth district. Mail was carried on some routes: Callington to Saltash being one example. One bus broke its driving shaft at Burraton, just west of Saltash, and the problem of getting the Royal Mail, railway parcels and passengers to Saltash was solved when a passing empty hearse offered to assist!

To ease the petrol shortage during the First World War, some GWR buses were converted to run on coal gas; an inner bag of red rubber held the gas within an outer casing of rubber-treated canvas, placed either on the roof of a single-deck vehicle or replacing some outside seats on a double-deck bus.

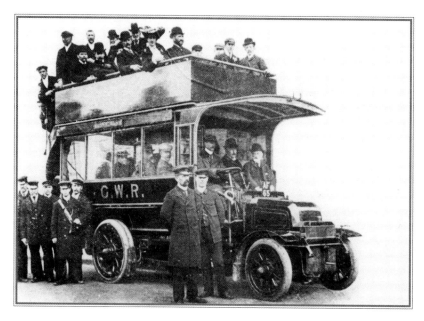

Outside Penzance station is the first GWR double-decker bus. No. 6, registration AF 65, it was built by Milnes Daimler with a 20 hp engine. Note the rear brakes consisting of wooden brake shoes acting directly on the solid rubber tyres. When descending a long hill with a full load the tyres were often known to smoulder, or even ignite!

1904 Author's collection

GWR twenty-two-seat 16 hp Milnes Daimler for the Lizard waiting to leave Helston station. This bus had been purchased from the Lynton & Barnstaple Railway.

17.8.03 Author's collection

An innovation in 1927 was the introduction of road-rail tickets between common points whereby a forward journey by one method of transport could be used for a return journey by the other. In 1928 there was the first GWR six-day 'Land Cruise' in the West of England. Starting at Bath, it passed through Cheddar and Exmoor to Torquay returning via Dartmoor, East Devon and Hardy's Wessex back to Bath.

The LSWR worked a less-extensive bus service than the GWR, but was an early operator. Its first motor bus service started on 1 June 1903 between Exeter Queen Street station and Chagford using two Milnes-Daimler single-deckers. Short workings were run to Crockernwell. Wisely, advance arrangements were made for horse brakes to be supplied in the event of a mechanical failure. In 1905 the service used Clarkson steam buses and the Locomotive Superintendent ruled that as they were steam driven, they must be maintained at Exmouth Junction locomotive depot. In 1908 these vehicles were replaced by Thornycroft petrol buses. After the First World War pirate buses undercutting LSWR fares siphoned off traffic to such an extent that the service ran at a loss and was therefore withdrawn on 20 September 1924.

The first GWR bus at Weymouth ran on 16 June 1905. From 22 July 1912 the GWR and LSWR operated joint bus services in the area. Although expenses and profits were shared, maintenance was carried out entirely by the GWR. Under Parliamentary powers, from 1928 legislation permitted railways to buy large, but not controlling, shareholdings in existing bus companies. The GWR and SR reached agreement with the National Omnibus & Transport Company. The Western National was set up to run bus services in GWR territory, the railway agreeing to transfer its road motor services to that company in return for a half share, the Western National undertaking to co-ordinate rail and road services and not compete with the railway. The Southern National operated similar services in SR areas. The GWR and SR took a half share (GWR 30 per cent and SR 20 per cent) in the Devon General Omnibus & Touring Company. On 1 January 1934 the final railway service taken over by the Southern National was the joint service at Weymouth. Through their 'National Omnibus' associations, the GWR and SR acquired interest in 'Royal Blue' long-distance coach services previously operated by Elliott Brothers and connecting Dorset, Devon and Cornwall with London. The GWR also owned shares in the Bristol Tramways & Carriage Company.

Sealink bus and luggage trailer in Weymouth station forecourt working the service to the quay. Note the logo 'Western National', the owner of the vehicle.

7.8.81 Author

## ROAD TRANSPORT FOR GOODS

Although the GWR used horse-drawn lorries and vans throughout its life, a policy continued by BR into the early 1950s, this method of collection and delivery was used principally within a radius of a couple of miles around the railhead. Very heavy goods were unloaded from drays using cartage skids. These were two lengths of wood about 7 ft long, with a hook at one end to catch on the side of the dray, the other end resting on the ground. Chains kept the lengths from spreading too wide apart. In the 1940s horses were still found to be more economic than a mechanical vehicle for a 3-mile round trip.

| Distance in miles | Horse van/lorry | 2-ton motor lorry | 4-ton motor lorry | 3-ton mechanical horse |
|---|---|---|---|---|
| ¼ | 10d | 1s 5d | 1s 9d | 1s ¼d |
| ½ | 11¾d | 1s 6d | 1s 10d | 1s 1d |
| 1 | 1s 2d | 1s 8d | 1s 11d | 1s 2½d |
| 1½ | 1s 4d | 1s 10d | 2s 1¼d | 1s 3¾d |

Crates of broccoli being loaded into open wagons at Penzance from a GWR lorry which has white wing tips to provide better visibility during Second World War blackouts.

April 1942 Author's collection

Country collection and delivery was by motor van or lorry. The country lorry service catered both for goods depot traffic and passenger parcels, smaller stations being serviced by a vehicle based at a nearby larger station. Some traffic needed specialized vehicles such as for livestock, sugar beet or timber. For beet the GWR used a Fordson tractor hauling a trailer, Swindon supplying special sugar-beet forks whose 9 tines had bulbous ends to prevent the beet from being damaged. The railway supplied vehicles for taking livestock and machinery to and from county shows such as the Bath and West and the Royal Cornwall. Some vehicles owned by the GWR and driven by its staff were on contract hire to biscuit and chocolate companies and painted in the livery of the hiring firm. This scheme enabled a firm's products to be carried on the long haul by rail and then delivered locally by road from the railhead store.

Until 1947, GWR 'smalls' traffic was carried on rail in station trucks – a four-wheeled goods van usually coupled near the engine and unloaded at passenger-station platforms. That year most station truck working was abolished and replaced by zonal collection and delivery by road from large centres such as Taunton, Exeter or Plymouth, smaller stations only dealing with full wagon loads and private siding traffic. This proved an economic move.

## RAILWAY AIR SERVICES

On 21 May 1929 the 'Big Four' railway companies obtained Parliamentary powers enabling them to operate air services. The GWR was the first company to take the initiative and on 12 April 1933 opened a service between Cardiff, Haldon (sited just inland from Dawlish and serving Teignmouth and Torquay) and Plymouth. The machine used, a three-engined, six-seater Westland Wessex, built appropriately in GWR territory at Yeovil, was painted in chocolate and cream livery. Its interior décor was similar to a standard first-class compartment. Imperial Airways Limited supplied the plane, pilot and ground staff for the twice-daily flights. It took about fifty minutes to cover the 80 miles, compared with almost four hours and 140 miles by rail. The GWR provided buses to connect with Cardiff General, Torquay and Plymouth North Road stations and the enquiry bureau at Teignmouth Town Hall. On 22 May 1933 one service each way was extended to Birmingham.

| Birmingham to: | Time by rail between stations | Time between airports | Single fare | |
|---|---|---|---|---|
| | | | rail | air |
| | | | £ s d | £ s d |
| Cardiff | 170 mins | 70 mins | 1 2 6 | 2 0 0 |
| Torquay | 298 mins | 140 mins | 1 19 10 | 2 10 0 |
| Plymouth | 320 mins | 170 mins | 2 5 3 | 3 0 0 |

From 15 May 1933 the GWR received permission from the Postmaster General to carry mail on the service. Letters were required to be handed in at a GWR air

Westland 'Wessex' aircraft hired from Imperial Airways and painted in GWR livery with the railway's coat-of-arms on the tail.

1933 Author's collection

booking office and on arrival at the airport at the end of the flight were posted for delivery in the ordinary way. A special GWR airmail stamp costing 3*d* had to be fixed in addition to the ordinary 1½*d* GPO stamp. When the seasonal service ended on 30 September 1933 only 714 passengers had been carried by air and the operation lost £6,526.

In 1934 the four main line railway companies in association with Imperial Airways formed the Railway Air Services Limited and this re-started the former GWR service on 7 May 1934 using a two-engined, eight-seater De Haviland Dragon, the service being extended to Speke, Liverpool. As in the previous year, it only operated from May until September. From 1936 the RAS ran a Bristol–Weston-super-Mare–Cardiff–Haldon–Plymouth service, Haldon being a request stop. The service was permanently withdrawn on 3 September 1939.

## PRESERVED RAILWAYS

In the 1960s, the Beeching Report, followed by the closure of many branch lines and the withdrawal of steam traction, led most people to believe that such things were gone for ever. Preservationists thought otherwise and a variety of lines survived to enable tourists still to enjoy the sight, sound and smell of steam amid glorious scenery.

The Paignton & Dartmouth Steam Railway offers splendid sea and river visitas combined with hard-working locomotives on stiff gradients, while a ride on the South Devon Steam Railway from Buckfastleigh to Totnes offers a branch line meandering along the valley floor beside the River Dart. These two lines are ex-GWR, but the Swanage Railway allows an ex-SR branch line to be savoured, and moreover, a branch line capable of taking main line locomotives. The West Somerset Railway is an ex-GWR branch which can also take main line engines and at 20 miles in length is the longest

4–6–0 No. 7827 *Lydham Manor* at Kingswear on the Paignton & Dartmouth Steam Railway.
May 1985 W.H. Harbor/C.G. Maggs's collection

Bishops Lydeard Down platform from the fireman's side of the cab of '5101' class 2–6–2T No. 4160 preserved on the West Somerset Railway. Note the fire-irons along the top of the tank.

30.7.96 Author

'5101' class 2–6–2T No. 4160 at Bishops Lydeard heading the 12.20 p.m. to Minehead.

30.7.96 Author

'64XX' class 0–6–0PT No. 6412 at Buckfastleigh on the Dart Valley Light Railway.

April 1970 W.H. Harbor/C.G. Maggs's collection

BR Standard Class 4MT 4–6–0 No. 75029 *The Green Knight*, built at Swindon in 1954, giving brake van rides at Cranmore on the East Somerset Railway. A fine replica GWR engine shed has been built to house the locomotive stock.

April 1976 W.H. Harbor/C.G. Maggs's collection

preserved line in Britain. Shorter lines are the East Somerset Railway which runs under the south side of the Mendip Hills and the Bodmin & Wenford Railway offering a 6½-mile ride through beautiful Cornish countryside. This line is particularly interesting as it carries freight in addition to passengers. There is a weekly exchange of Fitzgerald Lighting traffic with the English, Welsh & Scottish Railway at Bodmin Parkway, usually two VGAs each to St Helens and Edinburgh, while timber traffic is a probability and in the longer term it is hoped to relay the line to Wenford Bridge to carry English China Clay traffic.

The Somerset & Avon Railway hopes to re-open the line between Radstock and Frome. The Plym Valley Railway has its headquarters at Marsh Mills where a new station has been built about 200 yd north of the original. The ½-mile long line to World's End opened at Easter 1998. Other short lines operate at the Bristol Industrial Museum and Yeovil Junction. This latter line is a little different: the South West Main Line Steam Company is the outcome of an attempt to prevent the removal of the turntable at Yeovil Junction which would have ended main line steam there. The company leased land including the Down island platform, Clifton Maybank spur and the turntable. Plans are currently being made to re-open the Weymouth Quay line by integrating it into a

A 'Santa Special' at Bodmin General on the Bodmin & Wenford Railway. At its head is Bagnall 0–4–0ST *Alfred* built in 1953 for use on the Port of Par lines. The unusually low profile was essential as it ran in a low tunnel below the GWR main line.

December 1990 David Horne

Robert Stephenson & Hawthorn 0–6–0T, built in 1949, heads a 'Mince Pie Rambler' train at Bodmin General station on the Bodmin & Wenford Railway. Until 1971 this engine shunted at Hertfordshire power stations.

31.12.95 David Horne

Ex-GWR 0–6–0PT No. 7752 on loan from the Birmingham Railway Museum runs round a replica clay train at Bodmin Parkway on the Bodmin & Wenford Railway's annual steam gala.

10.9.94 David Horne

circular route to be formed by laying track along the Esplanade, Promenade and King Street. The system would link rail and bus stations, car parks and shopping streets. Parry 'People Mover' trams are envisaged, each car to be driven by an on-board flywheel which would be plugged into a roadside power point to replace spent energy every two or three stops.

Apart from these standard gauge lines, some of narrow gauge have been laid on former standard gauge formations. Perhaps the most impressive of these is the 2 ft 9 in gauge Seaton Tramway which runs beside the estuary of the River Axe for 2 miles and then passes through pleasant rural scenery for a further mile. The 1 ft 11½ in gauge Launceston Steam Railway runs to Newmills and the 2 ft gauge Gartell Light Railway is laid on the Somerset & Dorset Railway formation just south of Templecombe. The Lynton & Barnstaple Railway Association has purchased Woody Bay station and hopes to relay track between there and Parracombe. Not a preserved line as such, but worthy of mention, is the 1 ft 6 in gauge Bicton Woodland Railway, East Budleigh, which uses rolling stock from Woolwich Arsenal.

# MAIN LINES: GWR

Although the main line from Paddington to Penzance was considered a single entity, it was built by several railway companies. The Great Western Railway opened throughout from Paddington to Bristol on 30 June 1841, but the line further west was constructed by separate companies which were absorbed by the GWR in due course. The Bristol & Exeter opened to Exeter on 1 May 1844; the South Devon to Plymouth on 5 May 1848. After a wait of eleven years the Cornwall Railway took the line on to Truro on 4 May 1859. Meanwhile, the West Cornwall Railway had been authorized to rebuild the Hayle Railway and extend it to Truro and Penzance, the latter being reached on 11 March 1852, with through communication with Truro on 25 August 1855.

As the West Cornwall Railway was built to the standard gauge, through traffic had to be transferred at Truro. This caused delay, inconvenience and expense, so in 1864 the Cornwall Railway exercised its powers to insist that the broad gauge be laid. As the West Cornwall had insufficient funds to do this, the Associated Companies – the GWR, B&ER and the SDR – took over the West Cornwall from 1 July 1865. Broad gauge goods trains ran to Penzance from 6 November 1866 and passenger trains on this gauge from 1 March 1867. Subsequently the GWR absorbed the B&ER on 1 July 1876 and the SDR and the Cornwall Railway a month later.

The coming of the railway to the West of England resulted in the abolition of the practice of keeping local time. A note in the early timetables stated that 'London time is kept at all stations on the railway, which is about 11 minutes before Bristol and Bath time and 14 minutes before Bridgwater time'. As the use of two times proved confusing, Greenwich time replaced local time, but only after prolonged struggle on behalf of local custom. Bristol adopted Greenwich time on 14 September 1852.

One episode in I.K. Brunel's life which his admirers would prefer forgotten was his use of the locomotive-less atmosphere propulsion. A 15 in diameter cast-iron pipe was laid between the rails, air from it being exhausted by stationary steam pumps. A piston travelled in the pipe and to enable the piston to be connected to a special carriage to which a train could be coupled, the top of the pipe had a continuous slit closed by a leather flap. One edge of this longitudinal valve formed a hinge, while the other was sealed with grease to make it air tight, a roller behind the piston re-sealing this valve. As the air in front of the piston had been pumped out, the atmosphere pressure behind the piston pushed it forward and the carriage and train, leaving the valve closed and the pipe ready to be exhausted for the next train.

This system had several advantages over locomotive haulage: collisions on a single line were impossible; there was no nuisance from coke dust and speeds were higher than those obtained using conventional haulage.

Initially the system proved successful, but then problems abounded: the leather valve did not make an air-tight seal; the leather deteriorated; the pumping engines were inefficient and unreliable; the proposed telegraph between the pump houses was not installed so fuel was wasted when pumps exhausted air on time for a train which proved to be late. Atmospheric traction continued after a fashion for eight months but was then abandoned in favour of conventional locomotive working. At a cost of nearly £½ million the 'Atmospheric Caper' saddled the SDR with 40 miles of single line and a set of gradients which are a problem to this day.

Apart from the GWR's main line to the west, it also owned an important cross-country route. The Wilts, Somerset & Weymouth Railway linked the London to Bristol main line at Thingley Junction, and also at Bathampton with Salisbury and Weymouth, Salisbury being reached on 30 June 1856 and Weymouth on 20 January 1857. With the opening of the Severn Tunnel in 1886 and the introduction of through trains between South Wales, Bristol and Portsmouth, the Salisbury branch became a main line, while the development of Channel Islands traffic made Weymouth important. The former GWR route from Castle Cary to Weymouth has been relegated to branch status, part of it reduced to single track in 1968.

In the early years of the twentieth century, critics of the GWR claimed that its initials stood for 'Great Way Round' and certainly some of its main routes were far from bee lines. Travelling to Exeter via Bristol was definitely a diversion and, as it was only 15 miles from Castle Cary on the Wilts, Somerset & Weymouth Railway to Langport on the Taunton to Yeovil branch, it meant that for the cost of only 15 miles of line, and the Durston by-pass, a new, shorter route to the West could be made saving 20 miles over the route via Swindon and Bristol. Bridges were strengthened, the line doubled and some of the sharper curves between Reading, Newbury and Savernake re-aligned, while a cut-off from Patney & Chirton to Westbury avoided the detour through Devizes. This opened to goods on 29 July 1900 and passengers on 1 October 1900, reducing the distance to Weymouth by 14 miles. The new Castle Cary to Langport line opened to goods on 11 June 1906 and to passengers on 1 July 1906. The route was further improved in March 1933 by opening the Westbury and Frome avoiding lines, by-passing 30 mph speed restrictions thus saving five minutes and at least a ton of coal a day, quite apart from wear and tear.

An improvement completed in 1932 was quadrupling the line from Cogload Junction to Norton Fitzwarren, thus easing the Taunton bottleneck. A flyover was constructed at Cogload Junction to avoid delays caused by the surface crossing.

The early years of the twentieth century were renowned for increased speed. On 7 March 1902 King Edward VII and Queen Alexandra travelled to Dartmouth to lay the foundation stone of the Royal Naval College. The 228½ miles from Paddington to Kingswear via Bristol were covered in 4 hours 22½ minutes, the longest GWR non-stop run to date. Three days later the record was beaten when the royal couple returned from Plymouth to Paddington, the 246½ miles from Millbay Junction being covered in 4 hours 24 minutes. On 14 July 1903 the Prince and Princess of Wales travelled behind 4-4-0 *City of Bath* from Paddington to Plymouth, North Road in only 3 hours 53½ minutes and arrived 37½ minutes before they were expected. This time included easing the speed between Tiverton Junction and Exeter while the royal party was at lunch and a reduction of speed for tablet exchange on the then single line between Dawlish and Teignmouth. The 1 in 36 gradient of Dainton Bank only slowed the train to a minimum of 30 mph, while the lowest speed on Rattery Bank was 36 mph. The train averaged 67 mph from Paddington to Exeter and 51 mph between Exeter and Plymouth, North Road.

In the first decade of this century, competition for Plymouth liner traffic caused racing between the GWR and LSWR. The latter's fastest time was on 23 April 1904 when the 230 miles were covered in 4 hours 3 minutes, but this was eclipsed by the GWR on 9 May when its longer route of 246½ miles was run in 3 hours 47 minutes; the 4–4–0 *City of Truro* working the Plymouth to Bristol leg achieving a world record of 102.3 mph down Wellington Bank. Although it has since been proved that the observer Rous-Marten's times were not absolutely accurate, that great student of locomotive running, O.S. Nock, studied the figures exhaustively and was convinced that the *City of Truro* reached at least 100 mph.

Nationalization in 1948 meant that most GWR lines became the Western Region and those of the Southern Railway, the Southern Region. Under privatization the West of England is served by Great Western Trains to and from London; Virgin Cross Country for the Midlands and beyond. Wales & West Railway operates Alphaline services and the region's branch lines, while South West Trains operates to and from Waterloo.

There were in excess of 100 steam sheds situated in major towns and also at the junction or terminus of almost every branch line, together with the many carriage and wagon depots. These have been reduced to: traction and rolling stock maintenance depots at Bournemouth; St Philip's Marsh, Bristol; Penzance and Plymouth; a traction and maintenance depot at Salisbury and a carriage and wagon maintenance depot at Barton Hill, Bristol.

The gradients between Bath and Taunton are insignificant, but on the direct West of England line via Westbury there is a descent in West Wiltshire from Savernake to Lavington which caused problems to Up trains, particularly if heavy or hauled by an engine shy for steam. West of Frome, Brewham Summit is approached from both directions at gradients of about 1 in 100. The line undulates to Taunton and then beyond Wellington climbs on a ruling gradient of 1 to 80 to Whiteball signal-box, descending more gently to Exeter.

From Aller Junction, west of Newton Abbot, where the Torbay line leaves, is an ascent at a maximum of 1 in 36 – very steep for a British main line – to Dainton signal-box, followed by a descent to Totnes. From there the line climbs Rattery Bank on a ruling gradient of 1 in 47 to Marley Tunnel, from where the line rises at a less severe gradient to Wrangaton, followed by a descent, particularly steep at 1 in 42 for the 1½ miles between Hemerdon and Plympton. From Plymouth to Penzance the undulating line is on an almost constant gradient, the longest length of level line being the final 1¾ miles before reaching Penzance.

Charles Rous-Marten in the *Railway Magazine*, March 1902, commented on the completion of No. 100, the first GWR express passenger 4–6–0:

It is the special difficulty of the Great Western Railway that its worst banks do not lie within compact limits, like that of the London & North Western Railway at Shap, or those of the Caledonian at Beattock and Dunblane, which can be conveniently worked with the aid of a bank engine stationed at the foot. From Newton Abbot to Penzance, a distance of 112½ miles, there is hardly a single level stretch of any material length. Putting aside the relatively easy bit across the tableland extending between Rattery and Hemerdon summits, about 12 miles, the road is a series of perpetually recurrent steep-sided gables, far severer than the Shap, Beattock, Dunblane, Falahill, Whitrope, or Barrhead inclines, or than the grades by which the London and South Western crosses Dartmoor; worse even, on the average, than those of the Aviemore–Culloden cut on the Highland line.

The West of England certainly had its share of named passenger trains. 'The Flying Dutchman' was named after the 1849 Derby and St Leger winner. This express began running four years earlier when it took 5 hours to complete the 194 miles between Paddington and Exeter, the route, of course, going via Bristol. In December 1847 it was speeded to 4 hours 25 minutes, making it the fastest train in the world, but six years later it ran to a considerably easier schedule.

LSWR competition in 1862 brought a train over the 171½ miles between Waterloo and Exeter in 4¾ hours, 25 minutes faster than the Bristol & Exeter could manage. The broad gauge counteracted by speeding 'The Flying Dutchman' to 4½ hours. Nine years later the LSWR introduced a 4½ hour schedule causing the GWR to retime the 'Dutchman' to reach Exeter in only 4¼ hours. In 1874 the 2.10 p.m. ex-Waterloo, frequently referred to as the 'Beeswing', arrived at Exeter in 4¼ hours. By 1879 the LSWR ran to Exeter in 4 hours and, furthermore, carried third-class passengers, a group of people which hitherto the broad gauge companies thought unworthy to carry at speed. To prevent too many passengers diverting to a rival company, the GWR introduced the standard gauge 'Zulu' which reached Exeter in 4 hours 14 minutes. The 'Dutchman' did not accommodate third-class passengers until 1890.

Following the abolition of the compulsory 10-minute refreshment stop at Swindon, in 1896 the Newquay portion of the 'Cornishman' ran non-stop from Paddington to Exeter in 3¾ hours, easily making it the world's longest railway journey not calling at a station. In 1903 the time was reduced to 3½ hours.

In 1904 the GWR introduced the 'Cornish Riviera Express' which made a non-stop run to Plymouth, North Road in 4 hours 25 minutes, while in 1906 the combination of newer engines and a shorter route cut the time to 4 hours 7 minutes. The 'Cornish Riviera Express' also carried slip coach portions detached at Westbury for Weymouth; Taunton for Minehead and Ilfracombe; and at Exeter for Torquay. This made the train progressively lighter as it reached the steeper gradients. By 1939 the 'Cornish Riviera Express' consisted of eight through portions during the summer: the main train to Penzance; two slip coaches for Weymouth; through coaches for Minehead and Ilfracombe; and coaches for Kingsbridge, Newquay, Falmouth and St Ives. On summer Saturdays separate trains were run to these destinations. Diesel traction permitted times of 3½ hours to Plymouth and 5 hours 35 minutes to Penzance. In 1997 the fastest train over the 305¼ miles between Paddington and Penzance took only 4 hours 55 minutes compared with the 6 hours 25 minutes of 1939. The reduction would have been greater but for the fact that the line is subject to many speed restrictions due to curves and viaducts.

Other Western Region named trains have included 'The Mayflower' and 'The Golden Hind' between Paddington and Plymouth, and 'The Royal Duchy', Paddington to Penzance; and 'The Torbay Express', Paddington to Kingswear. The 'Torquay Pullman' ran between Paddington and Paignton in 1929, but was withdrawn the following year. Some through trains to and from the Midlands were named. 'The Devonian' was the first and in 1927 ran between Bradford and Bristol, three coaches being handed over to the GWR for continuation to Paignton. In 1952 'The Cornishman' ran between Wolverhampton and Penzance, a name formerly used from Paddington.

Today's named trains do not have the glamour of the roof-boarded named trains of earlier years and all work on the North to South West route.

| Name | Route |
|------|-------|
| 'The Armada' | Leeds to Plymouth |
| 'The Devonian' | Leeds to Paignton |
| 'The Cornishman' | Dundee to Penzance (12 hours 15 minutes) |
| 'The Cornish Scot' | Edinburgh to Penzance |
| 'The Devon Scot' | Aberdeen to Plymouth (11 hours 16 minutes) |
| 'The Night Riviera' | Waterloo to Penzance |
| 'The Pines Express' | Manchester to Bournemouth |

Unfortunately there have been several serious accidents in Somerset and Wiltshire, but not a single passenger has ever been killed in Devon and Cornwall. One serious accident did occur in Cornwall, but proved fatal only to railway staff. Trains on the Cornwall Railway were started by word of mouth as the only signals were 'homes' for admitting a train into a station. On 2 December 1873 two goods trains were waiting in the passing loop at Menheniot. On receiving 'Line Clear' for the Down train, the porter-signalman called out 'Right away, Dick'. To his horror the Up double-headed goods drew away because, unknown to him, the other guard's name was also Dick. The Up goods and another Down goods crashed together on a sharp curve in a cutting. One driver was killed and all three engine crews badly injured. This accident led to the immediate installation of starting signals throughout the line.

Two very serious accidents occurred at Norton Fitzwarren, the second almost exactly fifty years after the first. On 11 November 1890 a broad gauge 4–4–0ST hauling passengers and mail from a South-African liner ran headlong into a Down standard gauge goods train shunted on to the Up line and forgotten by the signalman. Ten passengers were killed. To prevent a repetition, Rule 55 was adopted by all British railways. It ordered that when a train halted at a signal the driver was to sound his whistle, and if the signalman did not lower his board after three minutes the driver was required to send to the signal-box to inform the 'bobby' of the train's presence, and not leave until a collar had been placed over the relevant levers to prevent a conflicting movement being made.

In the wartime blackout on 4 November 1940, breaking with the usual custom, the 9.50 p.m. Paddington to Penzance sleeper was sent from Taunton to Norton Fitzwarren on the Down Relief line. The driver failed to realize this in the blackout, mistook the main line signals for his own and was derailed at the trap points killing twenty-seven passengers.

The vicinity of Taunton was once again the scene of a tragedy when on 5 July 1978 twelve passengers on the 21.30 Penzance to Paddington sleeper were killed by poisonous fumes given off by burning material. Several recommendations were made to prevent a repetition, including the suggestions that polyurethane mattresses be removed and fire-retardant bed linen used.

The Photographs in this and subsequent sections are generally in east
to west order.

## BRISTOL & EXETER RAILWAY.

## CHEAP EXCURSION

TO

## WESTON.

On MONDAY, MAY 31st, 1869,

## A CHEAP EXCURSION

WILL RUN AS UNDER.

FARES TO AND FRO,
on this occasion,
COV. CARS.

| LEAVING | A.M. | |
|---|---|---|
| Exeter | 8. 0 | |
| Hele and Bradninch | 8.23 | |
| Collumpton | 8.35 | **1s. 6d.** |
| Tiverton Junction | 8.44 | |
| Tiverton | 8. 0 | |
| Wellington | 9. 7 | |

Arriving at Weston about 10.30 a.m.   Returning from Weston at 6 p.m.

*The Tickets are not transferable, and are not available by any other Train or for any other Station.*

NO LUGGAGE ALLOWED.

By order,

## HENRY DYKES,

Terminus, Bristol, May 17th, 1869.        SUPERINTENDENT.

Exeter: Printed at the "Flying Post" Office, Little Queen Street.

A Bristol & Exeter Railway poster advertising
an excursion from Exeter to Weston-super-
Mare.

1869 Author's collection

'1366' class 0–6–0PT No. 1367 shunts sidings opposite Weymouth loco shed.

22.7.49 Pursey Short

Constructing the cut-off between Castle Cary and Langport and preparing the ground for the goods yard at Somerton.

1904 Author's collection

4–6–0 No. 5940 *Whitbourne Hall* passes Dorchester goods shed with the 4.35 p.m. Saturdays only Weymouth to Cardiff.

12.8.61 R.A. Lumber

'5101' class 2–6–2T No. 4113 between Bathampton and Limpley Stoke with the 5.18 p.m. Bristol Temple Meads to Trowbridge.

*c.* 1937 E.J.M. Hayward

'1366' class 0–6–0PT No. 1370 working a goods train on the Weymouth Quay tramway.

10.3.55 J.H. Bamsey

2R. 21778/16

THIS TRAIN RUNS ALONG THE PUBLIC ROADWAY BETWEEN THE QUAY AND THE JUNCTION WITH THE MAIN LINE AT WEYMOUTH. PASSENGERS ARE ASKED NOT TO USE THE LAVATORIES DURING THIS PART OF THE JOURNEY.

Poster displayed in toilet compartments of coaches running on the Weymouth Quay tramway.

*c.* 1960 Author's collection

No. 5067 *St Fagan's Castle* with the third part (Taunton and Minehead) of the 3.30 p.m. ex-Paddington, on the Frome avoiding line near Clink Road Junction.

*c.* 1937 E.J.M. Hayward

Interested spectators watch 4–6–0 No. 1007 *County of Brecknock* with a Paddington to Bristol express pass the Sydney Gardens, Bath.

4.9.51 Pursey Short

No. 6023 *King Edward II* picks up water from Keynsham troughs while working the 10.05 a.m. Bristol to Paddington. No. 6023 is preserved at Didcot Railway Centre.

11.6.57 Author

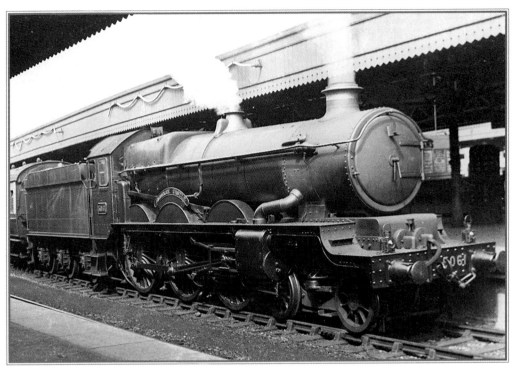

No. 5061 *Sudeley Castle* (later renamed *Earl of Birkenhead*) with the 3.50 p.m. Down express at Bristol Temple Meads; 'The Devonian' portion from the LMS is out of sight at the rear.

*c.* 1937 E.J.M. Hayward

A Paddington to Plymouth express behind No. 6014 *King Henry VII* passes Westbury North signal-box.

1952 Pursey Short

BR Standard Class 5MT 4–6–0 No. 73018 (70G Weymouth) at Westbury shed after working a perishable goods from Weymouth. To its right are Hymek D7041 and No. 6876 *Kingsland Grange*.

29.3.65 the Revd Alan Newman

'8750' class 0–6–0PTs No. 9790 and No. 3735 in Westbury shed.

30.8.65 the Revd Alan Newman

'8750' class 0–6–0PT No. 3681 just north of Dunball with a Highbridge to Tiverton Junction pick-up goods.

20.9.47 Pursey Short

'43XX' class 2–6–0 No. 7332 (83B Taunton) at its home shed. Piles of ashes can be seen on the ground. No. 7332 was built in 1932 as No. 9310. It had a heavy weight behind the buffer beam so that the pony truck would impart more side thrust to the main frames and bear a greater share of flange wear on severely curved routes. It was classified 'red'. By 1956 scrapping of earlier engines caused a shortage of 'blue' engines and so the '93XX' series had their weights removed between 1956 and 1959 and were re-numbered; this happened to 9310 in 1958.

24.10.63 the Revd Alan Newman

No. 5028 *Llantilio Castle* climbs Whiteball Bank with a Down express.

29.3.48 Pursey Short

'43XX' class 2–6–0 No. 7316 near Sampford Peverell with an Exeter to Taunton stopping train.

26.5.47 Pursey Short

4–6–0 No. 1028 *County of Warwick* at Exeter St David's with an Up express consisting of ex-LMS coaches.
The wall of the timber-built goods shed can be seen on the right.

*c.* 1954 P.Q. Treloar collection

No. 6018 *King Henry VI* enters Exeter St David's with the Royal train from Cornwall to London. The
Southern main line to Exeter Central rises on the left.

June 1951 T. Reardon

The 9.18 a.m. Saturdays only from Exmouth to Manchester, composed of a mixture of ex-GWR and LMS coaches, arrives at Exeter St David's behind No. 6959 *Peatling Hall.*

5.8.50 T. Reardon

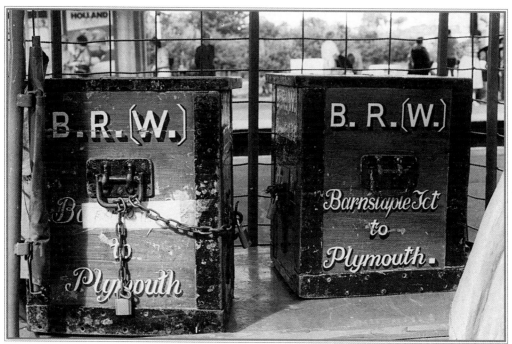

Travelling safes at Exeter St David's for the conveyance of booking-office cash: left, Exmouth to Plymouth and, right, Barnstaple Junction to Plymouth.

28.8.84 Author

The 1.30 p.m. Paddington to Paignton express, No. 186, hauled by mixed traffic '47XX' class 2–8–0 No. 4703 at Powderham, north of Starcross. These engines usually only appeared on express passenger workings on summer Saturdays.

16.7.49 Pursey Short

Newly painted in BR black-lined livery, No. 6966 *Witchingham Hall* leaves Starcross with an Exeter to Plymouth stopping train. On the left is a tower formerly part of the atmospheric railway pumping station. In the right-hand distance, the east bank of the River Exe estuary is visible.

24.3.51 Pursey Short

'90XX' class 4–4–0 No. 9023
nears Dawlish with a Down
goods.

*c.* 1950 M.E.J. Deane

An un-named, unidentified and grubby 'County' leaves Teignmouth along the sea wall with an Up express.

*c.* 1946 O.S. Nock/P.Q. Treloar's collection

'West Country' class Pacific No. 34001 *Exeter*, painted malachite green and its tender unlettered, leaves Dawlish with a Down stopping train. It was a regular SR duty to keep SR crews familiar with the WR route.

2.7.49 J.H. Bamsey

In blue livery No. 6008 *King James II* stands at Newton Abbot with an Up express.

*c.* 1950 O.S. Nock/P.Q. Treloar's collection

'14XX' class 0–4–2T No. 1466 (83A Newton Abbot) at its home shed. '57XX' class 0–6–0PT No. 5796 is on the left. No. 1466 is preserved at Didcot Railway Centre.

1.7.55 the Revd Alan Newman

No. 4099 *Kilgerran Castle* about to leave Kingswear with the 9.45 a.m. to Paddington. A clerestory coach is behind the tender – unusual on a post-Second World War express. Coal for Torquay gas works arrives at the quay by sea and is carried onwards by rail.

6.7.46 Pursey Short

BR Standard 'Britannia' class Pacific No. 70019 *Lightning* approaches Dainton Tunnel and Summit with the 9.30 a.m. Paddington to Falmouth express.

12.8.55 R.E. Toop

An Up goods behind '28XX' class 2–8–0 No. 2822 passes sidings at Dainton signal-box with '5101' class 2–6–2T No. 5153 assisting at the rear. The notice in the foreground reads: 'All Down goods and mineral trains with 35 wagons or less must stop dead here'.

27.6.50 Pursey Short

No. 6008 *King James II* nears Dainton Summit with the 'Cornish Riviera Express'. Despite evidence of poor condition, surplus steam is being emitted from the safety valves!

12.8.55 R.E. Toop

'3150' class 2–6–2T No. 3166 in the centre road, Totnes, bearing disc No. 3, and '48XX' class 0–4–2T No. 4867 at the Up platform with the Ashburton auto. The photograph was taken from the 5.30 a.m. Paddington to Penzance express standing at the Down platform.

1947 E.J.M. Hayward

North British diesel-hydraulic D6314 and No. 5034 *Corfe Castle* ascending Rattery Bank west of Totnes. Some coaches are painted maroon and others are brown and cream.

9.8.61 R.E. Toop

4–6–0 No. 6833 *Calcot Grange* with a Down goods train pauses at Dainton sidings signal-box.

12.8.55 R.E. Toop

No. 4914 *Cranmore Hall* ascends Rattery Bank with a Down goods banked in the rear by diesel-hydraulic D6327.

15.8.61 R.E. Toop

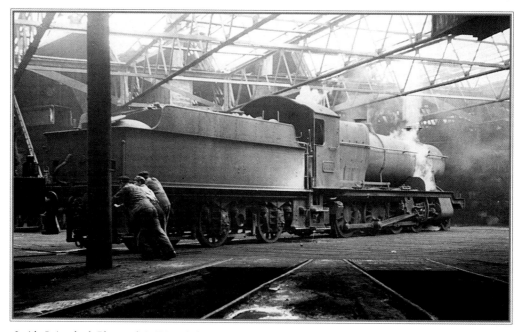

Inside Laira shed, Plymouth is '28XX' class 2–8–0 No. 3836 being turned with 3-man power. Note the flat deck and the wartime lack of side window in cab.

30.8.46 Pursey Short

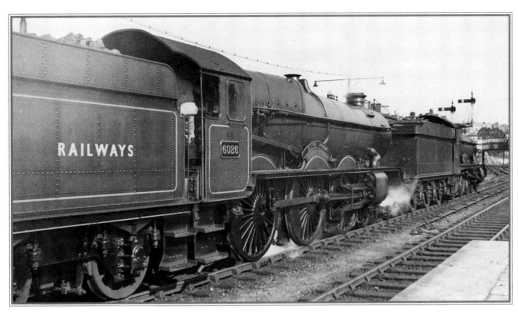

At Plymouth North Road an unidentified 'Hall' pilots a blue-liveried No. 6026 *King John* with an Up express.
*c.* 1950 O.S. Nock/P.Q. Treloar's collection

A BRUFF rail-road van at Plymouth Laira depot, which travels by road close to the scene of a de-railment and bumps over the running rails at right angles so that it sits astride them. The turntable slung below the lorry is lowered and the vehicle is swung round so that its four rubber-tyred road wheels are above the rails and then the van is lowered. At each of its outer ends a pair of flanged wheels keeps the rubber tyres on the rails.
6.4.93 Author

'51XX' class 2–6–2T No. 5148 at St Austell with a Down pick-up goods.

12.5.51 John Bamsey

No. 1023 *County of Oxford* climbs away from Truro with an Up express.

*c.* 1959 P.Q. Treloar

No. 6931 *Aldborough Hall*, on a summer's evening, leaves St Erth with an express for Penzance. The leading two coaches are non-corridor stock.

*c.* 1959 P.Q. Treloar

No. 4908 *Broome Hall* climbs from Hayle to Gwinear Road with the 10.20 a.m. Saturdays only Penzance to Swansea. Some of the coaches are ex-LMS stock.

26.7.56 P.Q. Treloar

No. 6801 *Aylburton Grange* brings an Up broccoli special into Gwinear Road.

April 1960 P.Q. Treloar

No. 4095 *Harlech Castle* pulls out of St Erth with an express to Penzance.

26.7.58 P.Q. Treloar

At Marazion No. 6870 *Bodicote Grange* with a broccoli special, is overtaken by No. 7929 *Wyke Hall* working an Up express.

April 1960 P.Q. Treloar

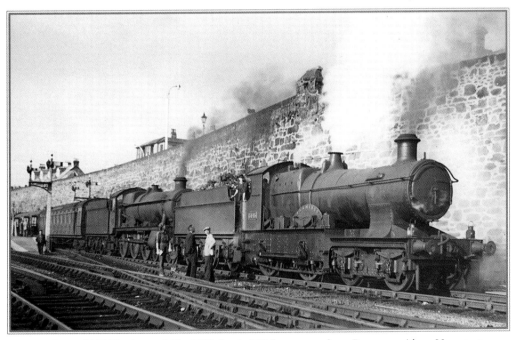

4–4–0 No. 3445 *Flamingo* and No. 5937 *Stanford Hall* prepare to leave Penzance with an Up express. *Flamingo* was withdrawn in December 1948.

*c.* 1948 O.S. Nock/P.Q. Treloar's collection

'45XX' class 2–6–2T No. 4547 arrives at Penzance with a stopping train from Truro. A 'Castle' heads the Up express.

*c.* 1957 R.A. Lumber

Outside Penzance station '94XX' class 0–6–0PT No. 9434 shunts 'The Royal Duchy' stock and the two Penzance to Glasgow coaches. The 'A' headlamp appears to be exhibited in error.

23.9.59 P.Q. Treloar

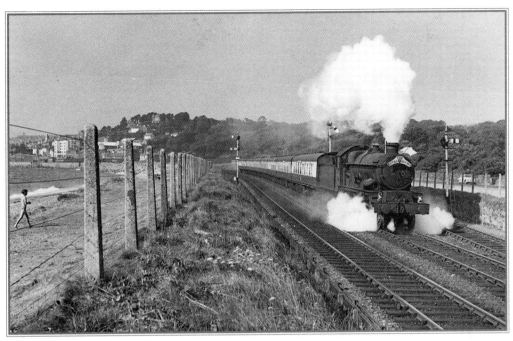

No. 7031 *Cromwell's Castle* with 'The Royal Duchy' to Paddington draws away from Penzance along the shore of Mount's Bay.

9.9.59 P.Q. Treloar

The accident at Norton Fitzwarren: right, standard gauge 'Standard Goods' class 0–6–0 No. 1100 with the goods train which had taken refuge on the Up line and left, broad gauge ex-B&ER 4–4–0ST No. 2051 at the head of the Plymouth to Paddington South African passenger and mail express.

11.11.1890 Author's collection

A 2–4–0T, with water to footplate level, passes through floods at Creech with an Up train. Note the windmill on the left.

*c.* 1887 Author's collection

A storm at Dawlish which breached the single track near the Down portal of Parson's Tunnel. Passengers from Up and Down trains pass round a temporary cliff path.

16.2.1855 Courtesy of *Illustrated London News*

A GWR poster advertising the delights of Cornwall.

*c.* 1906 Author's collection

Penzance station on the opening day of the West Cornwall Railway.

11.3.1852 Courtesy of *Illustrated London News*

# BRANCH LINES: GWR

With the opening of stations on the main line, traders, farmers and residents of towns not served by a railway could see the benefits they were missing. Strenuous efforts were often made to set up a local company to build a branch line. This was usually worked by a larger company because, although perhaps the line normally only required one engine and two passenger coaches, at least one other engine would be required as a spare to cover at times of boiler washout or extensive repair. On market days and bank holidays two coaches might prove insufficient. Some goods traffic required special rolling stock and it was uneconomic to invest capital in something used only occasionally. To obviate these difficulties, a small railway company usually arranged for a larger company with greater resources to work its line for a percentage of the gross receipts. Many of these branch lines were far from profitable, ordinary shareholders rarely, or never, receiving a dividend, and often the small railway was purchased by the working company for far less than it had cost to build.

Branch lines had to contend with bus competition from the 1920s, and road transport usually proved more convenient as passengers could board buses nearer their homes and be dropped close to their destinations, whereas railway stations tended to be built at locations convenient from the railway's point of view, quite often some distance from a village or town centre. To help combat this road competition, railways opened unstaffed halts at points near centres of population.

In addition to fighting bus competition, the increase in private-car ownership in the 1950s and '60s led to a further decline in the number of rail passengers and resulted in many branch lines in the West of England being closed by the 1963 Beeching Report, while those remaining tended to be passengers only or goods only. With the vast increase in road transportation, and the associated congestion and pollution, it is now considered that the closing of some branch lines was short sighted.

The GWR offered a wide variety of branches in the west. There were short branches like those to Clevedon and Ashburton running to a terminus. To avoid the time and trouble of uncoupling, running round and perhaps delaying main line traffic while doing so, and then recoupling, in the twentieth century such branches were often worked by steam railmotors or locomotive and auto trailer, both of which simply required a driver to walk from one end of the train to the other and then he was ready for the return journey.

Other branches, such as those to Minehead and Newquay were longer and offered through coaches, or even through trains, particularly on summer Saturdays. Another type of branch, such as Barnstaple to Norton Fitzwarren, and Exeter to Heathfield and Newton Abbot, connected one main line with another and on occasion could be used as an alternative route in the event of main line closure. Then there were mineral branches such as the many clay lines in Cornwall and the Limpley Stoke and Camerton line in North Somerset, which for most of its life was simply a goods and mineral branch.

Many of the former GWR branches were closed in the 1960s, but some remain, either in whole or truncated form, or as preserved lines for the enjoyment and edification of holidaymakers. The only former GWR branches still in use today as part of the main line passenger carrying system are found in Cornwall: the Looe, Newquay and St Ives branches. In addition there is the Newton Abbot to Paignton branch, formerly part of the main line to Kingswear. Branches in whole, or in part, still open to mineral traffic: in Somerset, the lines in the Frome area to Whatley and Merehead quarries; in Devon, the Marsh Barton branch at Exeter and the Heathfield line from Newton Abbot; while in Cornwall, the Fowey and Drinnick Mill branches.

The Weston, Clevedon & Portishead Light Railway, although never really part of the GWR, had physical links at Clevedon and Portishead for exchange of traffic and when it closed in 1940 the GWR purchased its assets with the view to using the line to store loaded coal wagons which had accumulated following the cessation of exports after the evacuation of Dunkirk. In the event only a few wagons were stored. The GWR scrapped all WC&PLR rolling stock and engines except for two ex-London, Brighton & South Coast Railway 'Terrier' 0–6–0Ts which it took into stock.

The WC&PLR enjoyed an eventful history. Although its Act was passed in 1885, due to financial difficulties the line from Weston to Clevedon was not opened until 1 December 1897 and did not reach Portishead until 7 August 1907. It usefully linked the three watering places by a far more direct route than that offered by the GWR. Most of the WC&PLR's level crossings were ungated and the number of signals minimal. The manager, Colonel H.F. Stephens, was innovative. In 1919 he manufactured concrete blocks to replace timber sleepers and to cut costs purchased a petrol railcar and also a shunting tractor in 1921. Then, when in the 1930s increased road traffic meant that some ungated level crossings had become particularly dangerous, these were protected by traffic lights. The stations had low-level platforms and the halts none at all. The original coaches were designed to give access from ground level and second-hand main line coaches purchased subsequently had steps added. After 1909 the company made no profit and a receiver was appointed. In 1940 a court order was made for the receiver to cease operating the line.

Near Watchet the West Somerset Mineral Railway ran very close to the GWR's Minehead branch, but was only linked by a temporary connection laid for transferring locomotives to or from the WSMR. The 13¼-mile-long line was constructed to carry iron ore from the Brendon Hills to Watchet from where it travelled by sea to South Wales for smelting. The WSMR's most notable feature was the opening on 31 May 1858 of an inclined plane, ¾ mile in length on a gradient of 1 in 4, which ranked among the longest and steepest in the country for standard gauge vehicles. Miners' trains were run from an early date, but a public passenger service did not start until 4 September 1865 and then only ran on the lower section between Combe Row and Watchet. No official passenger service was run up the incline, but passengers were allowed to travel free at their own risk. Early in 1879 all the mines closed and the passenger service halved. Trade revived in the autumn and three mines reopened only to close within four years. Traffic dwindled to such an extent that the line was completely closed on 7 November 1898. In March 1907 the Somerset Mineral Syndicate Limited was set up to reopen the mines. The first truckloads of ore descended the incline during that October, but a slump in the steel trade the following year caused the company to be wound up.

In December 1911 an Australian Company, A.R. Angus Limited, leased the line from Watchet to Washford to demonstrate its patent automatic train control. There were no signals, but an electric ramp between the rails showed a disc to the driver and blew a whistle. If the warnings were ignored, the regulator on the locomotive was automatically closed and the brakes applied. The system was demonstrated to representatives of all the principal main line companies but not adopted. The track was dismantled in 1917–18 for war service overseas. In September 1918 the line was resuscitated for the third time when the Timber Supply Department of the Board of Trade asked permission to lay a light railway from the government sawmills at Washford to the harbour at Watchet. Mules were used to pull the trucks and this line was lifted early in 1920, bringing the history of this fascinating railway to a close.

Chippenham, view Down: an auto coach and gas cylinder wagon for charging gas-lit coaches stand in the New-found-out Siding; a '48XX' class 0–4–2T and van are in the fish dock while a coach and vans stand in the parcels dock.

Easter 1937 M.J. Tozer collection

'14XX' class 0–4–2T No. 1433 near Hazeland Bridge working the 12.54 p.m. Chippenham to Calne.
25.10.55 Author

The west portal of Combe Hay Tunnel, formerly used by the Somerset Coal Canal.
20.7.52 Author

Footbridge at Monkton Combe, the ironwork of which was cast at Paulton in 1811 and formerly spanned the Somerset Coal Canal at the same location.

18.4.52 Author

The Liverpool & Manchester Railway 0–4–2 *Lion*, built 1838, in Monkton Combe goods yard. It has arrived for use in the film *The Titfield Thunderbolt*.

23.6.52 Author

'58XX' class 0–4–2T No. 5813 (82A Bristol, Bath Road) and brake van approach Wrington. The cows in the background have not wasted much time using the occupation crossing.

27.8.54 Author

'14XX' class 0–4–2T No. 1463 (82A Bristol, Bath Road) at Yatton with a train to Clevedon.

Easter Monday 1957 W.H. Harbor/C.G. Maggs's collection

Ivatt Class 2MT 2–6–2T No. 41207 arriving at Yatton with the last load of empty wagons from Clevedon, the goods depot there having closed on Saturday, 8 June 1963.

12.6.63 M. Wathen

Single line tablet for the section Yeovil Pen Mill to Yeovil Town.

Author

'64XX' class 0–6–0PT No. 6435 working the 16.30 Yeovil Pen Mill to Yeovil Town passing the coal stage and water tower of the former GWR shed which closed 5 January 1959. No. 6435 is preserved in the Paignton & Dartmouth Railway. Note the Southern Region upper quadrant signal.

9.8.64 R.A. Lumber

'45XX' class 2–6–2T No. 5504 (83B Taunton) on arrival at Taunton with the 9.15 a.m. Minehead to Taunton. The train consists of a strengthening corridor coach and a 'B' set. An auto coach stands on the right.

15.4.54 D. Holmes

'2251' class 0–6–0 No. 2261 (83B Taunton) at Minehead with a stopping train to Taunton.
24.8.51 the Revd Alan Newman

Cab view from '43XX' class 2–6–0 No. 7326 with the 4.10 p.m. Barnstaple Junction to Taunton. At South Molton passenger trains ran 'wrong road' whenever possible so that the platform adjoining the road approach was used. The platform on the left is built of timber for lightness as it is situated on an embankment.
9.8.63 Author

Ex-SR 'T9' class 4–4–0 No. 30710 on a Barnstaple Junction to Taunton train near Filleigh.

3.7.53 R.J. Sellick

'43XX' class 2–6–0 No. 6398 (83B Taunton) while working the 11.40 a.m. Taunton to Barnstaple goods became de-railed on Swimbridge catch points after running away. An 0–6–0PT has been moved to the far end of the train.

17.8.56 Author's collection

Driver Harold Hunt and Fireman Walt
Caddick beside '43XX' class 2–6–0
No. 6398 at Swimbridge while working a
Taunton to Barnstaple goods train.

*c.* 1960 Tony Harvey collection

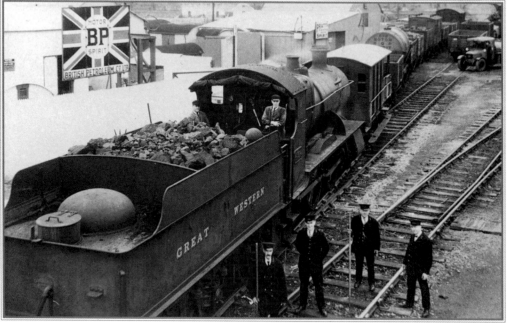

'43XX' class 2–6–0 No. 4304 at Barnstaple. In the distance, on the right, is a BP petrol lorry.

*c.* 1935 R.T. Clement collection

A Down Taunton to Ilfracombe express, headed by a '45XX' class 2–6–2T, at Acland Cross, east of Barnstaple.

*c.* 1928 A. Halls, courtesy of R.J. Sellick

'43XX' class 2–6–0 No. 7326 (83B Taunton) at Barnstaple Junction with the 4.10 p.m. to Taunton.

9.8.63 Author

'14XX' class 0–4–2T No. 1450 (83C Exeter) at Tiverton Junction. A rake of milk tanks, to or from Hemyock, can be seen in the background.

24.2.63 R.A. Lumber

'14XX' class 0–4–2T No. 1450, with the 12.42 p.m. from Tiverton Junction, approaches Tiverton pushing an auto trailer. On the left is a signal on the Exe Valley line. No. 1450 is preserved on the South Devon Railway.

8.6.63 Author

'14XX' class 0–4–2T No. 1421 at Hemyock with the 1.42 p.m. ex-Tiverton Junction. Unused on the Hemyock branch, the regulator control coupling for use on an auto train can be seen between the screw coupling and the heating pipe hose. Insufficient mileage was run to charge the batteries of this short-wheelbase ex-LNER coach, so it and its twin were run to Exeter once a fortnight.

8.6.63 Author

'45XX' class 2–6–2T No. 5573 at Brixham with a permanent way train.

7.8.60 R.E. Toop

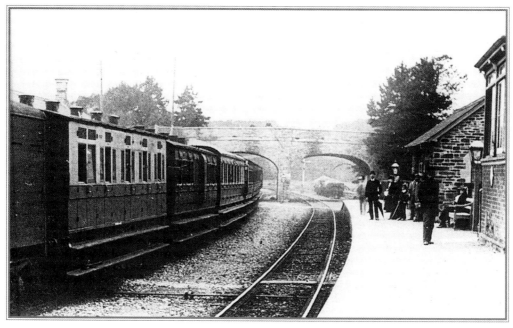

A train at Marsh Mills on the Launceston branch. The nearest two coaches were built in about 1875. Gauge conversion left a wide space between Down and Up loop lines.

*c.* 1900 Author's collection

A '44XX' class 2–6–2T, probably No. 4402, at the Princetown branch platform, Yelverton.

*c.* 1956 M.E.J. Deane

'45XX' class 2–6–2T No. 4542 on arrival at Princetown with two corridor coaches.

*c.* 1956 Lens of Sutton

Ivatt Class 2MT 2–6–2T No. 41283 at Launceston ex-GWR station, on arrival from Lydford, before reversing into the former LSWR station.

5.9.65 R.A. Lumber

'45XX' class 2–6–2T No. 4569 (83E St Blazey) at Bodmin Road (now Parkway) with a train for
Wadebridge.

*c.* 1956 P.Q. Treloar collection

'45XX' class 2–6–2T No. 4526 at Gaverigan Cross on the freight only Retew branch south of St Dennis
Junction.

1950 P.Q. Treloar collection

'42XX' class 2–8–0T No. 4273 and an unidentified 2–6–2T double-head a Cornish clay train.

*c.* 1950 P.Q. Treloar collection

View at Perranporth towards Truro with a 2–6–2T in the distance. As the platform is of the island variety – unusual for a branch station – for safety, passenger access was via a subway with egress up the steps on the other side of the fence to the right. In the left can be seen part of the concrete apron in front of the cattle pens. This enabled water used for washing the pens to drain away.

*c.* 1955 M.E.J. Deane

'45XX' class 2–6–2Ts No. 4564 and No. 4571 approach Lelant with the 9.20 a.m. St Ives to Paddington. The fifth vehicle is a restaurant car.

4.7.59 P.Q. Treloar

The unusual signal-box at Perranwell situated between the passenger platform and goods shed and above a goods siding.

c. 1960 Lens of Sutton

The first train arrives at Falmouth.

24.8.1863 Courtesy of *Illustrated London News*

'45XX' class 2–6–2T No. 4552 shunts a cattle wagon, used in this instance for transporting broccoli, at Nancegollan on the Helston branch.

*c.* 1960 P.Q. Treloar

'45XX' class 2–6–2T No. 4571 (83A Newton Abbot) shunting on the Hayle Wharf branch.

*c.* 1959 P.Q. Treloar

Brendon Hill incline on the West Somerset Mineral Railway.

20.4.1865 Author's collection

Ex-West Midland Railway No. 104, GWR 2–4–0 No. 213, was sold in 1911 to A.R. Angus to test his automatic train control system on the WSMR. It was sold to the Cambrian Railways in 1921, and then No. 213 was returned to the GWR in 1922 and was finally withdrawn in 1926.

*c*. 1912 Author's collection

'45XX' class 2–6–2T No. 4540 leaves the St Ives bay platform at St Erth.

*c*. 1958 P.Q. Treloar

# MAIN LINES: LSWR/SR

The LSWR first reached Salisbury via Eastleigh (then called Bishopstoke) on 27 January 1847, a direct line via Andover opening on 1 May 1857. The line was thrust westwards: on 18 July 1860 the LSWR directors left Waterloo in a twenty-coach special drawn by three engines and reached Exeter in 7 hours. The day was celebrated both by Exeter Fair and a total eclipse of the sun. A limited public service began the following day, full passenger services starting on 1 August and goods a month later. Thus far the LSWR had been south of the rival GWR, but west of Exeter positions were reversed giving rise to the curiosity at St David's station of GWR and LSWR trains to London running in opposite directions. Ilfracombe was reached on 20 July 1874, Plymouth on 18 May 1876 and Wadebridge on 27 March 1899. To expedite working, Yeovil Junction was remodelled with quadruple track in 1909, as was Seaton Junction in 1928.

From 1963 all lines west of Salisbury became part of the Western Region. As a result of this re-organization from 6 September 1964 the line decreased in importance as from that date all trains from Waterloo termina ted at Exeter and the reduction in traffic allowed sections of the line to be singled. West of Exeter the former main line between Meldon Quarry and Bere Alston closed on 6 May 1968, the section from Bere Alston to St Budeaux becoming part of the Calstock branch. In the 1990s through running was introduced between Waterloo and Paignton, and the Coleford Junction to Okehampton line saw passenger traffic again in the summer of 1997 when on Sundays only six trains ran each way between Exeter and Okehampton, some running through from Paignton and Exmouth. Although advertised locally, this service did not appear in the national timetable.

The LSWR main line between Salisbury and Exeter constantly undulates with a ruling gradient of 1 in 80, but generally the gradients are short and were capable of being rushed by through trains. The severest is the 6-mile climb, mostly at 1 in 80, from Seaton Junction to the west portal of Honiton Tunnel. The line was laid out by Joseph Locke in an age when the cost of building railways had increased and engineers were easily persuaded to save expense by going up and down hills rather than through them.

There is a rising gradient of 1 in 37 at Exeter between St David's and Central stations. Steam-hauled trains required an assisting locomotive either at the front or rear. A couple of Beyer Peacock double-framed 0–6–0 goods engines were involved in a comedy of errors on 15 November 1890. No. 241 stopped at St David's station with an Up ballast train. The regular banking engine had just become derailed so No. 223 was hastily summoned, but in the darkness, rain and general confusion the fireman of No. 223 forgot to couple to the rear brake van, so when the train moved off, contact was lost. Instead of wisely keeping well clear, Driver Clarkson on No. 223 attempted to buffer up, an almost impossible task under such conditions. To avoid too strong a bump, Clarkson sent his fireman along the running plate to the smokebox door to act as a lookout. Unfortunately, Clarkson, in an attempt to gain maximim visibility, leaned out too far, struck his head on the wall of St David's Tunnel and was knocked unconscious. In due course the train topped the bank and ran into Queen Street (as Central was then known) with the unattended engine merrily puffing away at the rear. The guards and crew of No. 241 attempted to bring the train to a halt but failed to do so until No. 223's fireman regained the footplate and closed the regulator. The following month's working timetables bore the notice: 'An engineman and his fireman have been fined £3 each for improper and careless banking between St David's and Queen Street stations, Exeter'.

The LSWR line left the GWR at Cowley Bridge Junction just north of Exeter and climbed steadily to Coleford Junction where the Plymouth line continued climbing, with several miles at 1 in 77, to a summit beyond Meldon Junction. The line then fell in a ruling gradient of 1 in 73 to the Taw Viaduct from where the line undulated to Plymouth.

From Coleford Junction the Barnstaple and Ilfracombe line rose to a summit at Copplestone before descending, mostly on gentle gradients, to Barnstaple. These easy grades continued beyond to Braunton where most trains took on banking assistance up the 4 miles of 1 in 40 to Mortehoe. From there the line descended, the last 2 miles at 1 in 36, to the station high above the town.

The LSWR ran no named trains to the West of England, but in 1926 the SR named the 11.00 a.m. from Waterloo the 'Atlantic Coast Express'. The name had been selected by competition, the winner being Guard Rowland. At times the 'Atlantic Coast Express' was the most multi-portioned train in the country, having no less than nine sections: for Lyme Regis, Seaton, Sidmouth, Ilfracombe, Torrington, Padstow, Bude, Plymouth and Exeter. In 1947 the all-Pullman 'Devon Belle' ran from Waterloo with up to ten cars for Ilfracombe and four for Plymouth. Due to lack of patronage it was withdrawn at the end of 1954. The train's special feature was a Pullman observation car at its rear.

The greatest LSWR disaster in the region took place at Salisbury on 1 July 1906 when an Up boat train from Plymouth ignored the 30 mph restriction round the sharp curve east of the station and tried to take it at 70 mph. Gravity caused it to topple over and strike a milk train passing on the Down line. Of the forty-three passengers, twenty-four were killed, as well as the footplate crew, the guard of the milk train and the fireman of a goods train standing nearby. Of the deceased, twenty-one were citizens of the USA and Queen Alexandra sent a message of sympathy to the USA ambassador. A memorial service was held in St Paul's Cathedral and a tablet erected in Salisbury Cathedral.

A line jointly owned by the LSWR and the Midland Railway was the Somerset & Dorset Joint Railway which linked Bournemouth and Bath. It proved a valuable through route between the Midlands and the south coast avoiding the GWR. The S&D began as a rail link from Burnham to Poole with ships crossing the Bristol and English Channels, but as large numbers of passengers seemed not to wish to travel from Cardiff to Cherbourg, a better idea to improve the S&D finances was an extension across the Mendips to Bath. This brought through traffic to the line and also tapped the Somerset coalfield. In 1927 a named train was introduced to the S&D. This was the 'Pines Express' from Manchester and Liverpool to Bournemouth. Although nominally an express, gradients and curves precluded fast running on many sections and the train was timed to take 2¼ hours for the 71 miles between Bath and Bournemouth making six intermediate stops.

It faced a 2-mile-long ascent at 1 in 50 out of Bath; then 8 miles, much at 1 in 50, to a summit at Masbury followed by an 8-mile descent, again mostly at 1 in 50, to Evercreech Junction. The line then undulated to Corfe Mullen Junction where it faced 1½ miles of rising 1 in 80 and a fall of 2 miles at 1 in 75, while beyond Poole was the 2-mile-long Parkstone Bank rising at 1 in 60. The 'Pines' was normally worked by an LMS engine and those not conversant with railways were surprised to see an LMS engine at Bournemouth whose geographical position could hardly be described as 'London', 'Midland' or 'Scottish'. On summer Saturdays in the 1950s a dozen of so through expresses ran over the S&D on their way between the north and Bournemouth. The beginning of the end of the S&D came on 8 September 1962 when the 'Pines' last ran over the S&D and all the other through trains were withdrawn. Local traffic was insufficient to make running economic and the line finally closed on 7 March 1966.

The S&D only had one accident which caused the death of passengers. This was on August Bank Holiday 1876 when due to carelessness, two trains were allowed on to the single line north of Radstock and twelve passengers were killed in the head-on smash.

The Up 'Bournemouth Belle' leaves Bournemouth West for Waterloo behind 'Merchant Navy' class Pacific No. 35013 *Blue Funnel*.

28.8.48 Pursey Short

The 1.30 p.m. Waterloo to Weymouth express hauled by 'Merchant Navy' class Pacific No. 35026 in blue livery, its nameplate *Lamport & Holt Line* covered, passes Weymouth shed.

22.7.49 Pursey Short

'Battle of Britain' class Pacific No. 34051 *Winston Churchill* at Salisbury shed bearing the 'Devon Belle' headboard. No. 34051 is preserved by the National Railway Museum.

28.6.54 the Revd Alan Newman

'West Country' class Pacific No. 34091 *Weymouth* near Tisbury with the 12.15 p.m. Portsmouth to Ilfracombe and Torrington.

4.8.62 Author

BR Standard Class 4MT 2–6–0 No. 76067 with the 11.10 a.m. Salisbury to Exeter approaches Buckhorn Weston Tunnel.

4.8.64 Author

'S15' class 4–6–0 No. 30841 passes Milborne Port station with a Down goods. Note the number of barrows. No. 30841 is preserved by the North Yorkshire Moors Railway.

30.6.50 Pursey Short

A Down stopping train leaves Yeovil Junction behind 'West Country' class Pacific No. 34009 *Lyme Regis*.

29.5.50 Pursey Short

'S15' class 4–6–0 No. 30831 at Yeovil Junction heads the 12.00 noon to Salisbury.

14.8.60 E. Wilmshurst

'S15' class 4–6–0 No. 30844 (72A Exmouth Junction) passes through Crewkerne with a Down goods.

7.7.51 Pursey Short

'S15' class 4–6–0 No. 30841 leaves Axminster with a Down train and passes below the bridge carrying the Lyme Regis branch.

2.8.58 South Western Circle Wessex Collection

The Up 'Devon Belle' passes Seaton Junction on the Up through road behind 'Merchant Navy' class Pacific No. 35008 *Orient Line*.

16.9.50 S.W. Baker

'King Arthur' class 4–6–0 No. 30744 *Maid of Astolat* leaves Sidmouth Junction with the 12.55 p.m. Exeter to Yeovil stopping train.

20.9.48 Pursey Short

'West Country' class Pacific No. 34048 *Crediton*, with its number painted unusually on the front buffer beam, has just backed on to the through 15.05 Exmouth and Sidmouth to Waterloo worked in from the branch by Hymek D7070 and North British D6312.

17.7.65 R.A. Lumber

The Down 'Devon Belle' between
Sidmouth Junction and Whimple
hauled by 'Merchant Navy' class
Pacific 21C8 *Orient Line*.
                20.9.48 Pursey Short

'West Country' class Pacific No. 34092 *City of Wells* enters Whimple with the 9.35 a.m. Yeovil Town to
Exeter Central. The station building is a typical Tite design. Notice the platform extension has been made at
a higher level. No. 34092 is preserved on the Keighley & Worth Valley Railway.
                12.4.64 R.A. Lumber

'West Country' class Pacific No. 21C109 *Lyme Regis* and 'Merchant Navy' class No. 21C3 *Royal Mail* in the coaling queue at Exmouth Junction shed.

30.8.46 Pursey Short

The new Exmouth Junction shed at about the time of its completion. Left to right are: 'S15' class 4–6–0 No. 827; 'H15' class 4–6–0 No. 491; 'L11' class 4–4–0 No. 438 and a superheated Drummond '700' class 0–6–0.

1928 Courtesy of the *Railway Engineer*

'Lord Nelson' class 4–6–0 No. 30861 *Lord Anson* passing St James' Park Halt with an Up Stephenson Locomotive Society special.

2.9.62 R.A. Lumber

GWR '43XX' class 2–6–0 No. 5376 and a 'West Country' class Pacific on the Down centre road at Exeter Central having worked together from Exmouth Junction shed. No. 5376 will take forward the Plymouth portion of the 3.00 p.m. ex-Waterloo, and the Pacific will take the Ilfracombe coaches.

*c.* 1947 Lens of Sutton

'West Country' class Pacific No. 34003 *Plymouth* leaves Exeter Central with the Up 'Atlantic Coast Express'.

19.8.51 R.A. Lumber

'N' class 2–6–0 No. 31851 leaves Platform 3 at Exeter St David's with a Plymouth Friary to Exmouth Junction goods.

*c*. 1960 T. Reardon

A feature of the 1950s was the operation of holiday expresses, passengers purchasing a ticket for several day excursions during one week. Here the 'City of Exeter Holiday Express' returns to Exeter St David's from Bude behind 'T9' class 4–4–0 No. 30709 and 'N' class 2–6–0 No. 31838.

30.7.58 T. Reardon

'West Country' class Pacific No. 34104 *Bere Alston* with a train for Exeter Central joins the ex-GWR main line at Cowley Bridge Junction. Note on the Down Barnstaple line the length of check rail, catch points and a permanent way 20 mph restriction board. The Down line from Taunton has a 50 mph restriction sign.

17.9.60 R.E. Toop

'N' class 2–6–0 No. 31859 passes Coleford Junction with an Up freight from Barnstaple.

26.3.64 R.A. Lumber

'West Country' class Pacific No. 34002 *Salisbury* leaving Barnstaple Junction for Ilfracombe. Note the angle at which it crosses the line to Torrington.

*c.* 1958 M.E.J. Deane

Ex-GWR '43XX' class 2–6–0 No. 6345 enters Barnstaple Junction with the 10.12 a.m. Ilfracombe to Cardiff.

15.8.64 E. Wilmshurst

Ivatt Class 2MT 2–6–2T No. 41297 station pilot, and 'West Country' class Pacific No. 34106 *Lydford* at Barnstaple Junction.

11.5.63 R.E. Toop

A summer Saturday Taunton to Ilfracombe express climbs Mortehoe bank behind ex-GWR '45XX' class 2–6–2T No. 5501 and banked by SR 'M7' class 0–4–4T No. 30036. To aid signalmen in the Taunton area a 'B' target indicated Barnstaple trains, and 'M' those to Minehead. The last two coaches of the six-coach train are ex-LMS vehicles. '

1.7.50 Pursey Short

'Battle of Britain' class Pacific No. 34074 *46 Squadron* (72A Exmouth Junction) at Ilfracombe with a train for Exeter Central. Note the horse box next to the engine.

22.8.61 South Western Circle Wessex Collection

The Up 'Devon Belle' arriving at Plymouth North Road from Friary station behind a gleaming 'West Country' class Pacific No. 21C103 *Plymouth*. The structure behind the locomotive's smoke box is the head of a lift shaft. Observe the train shed, later demolished in the station rebuilding programme.

8.8.47 Roger Venning

'N' class 2–6–0 No. 31846 (83D Exmouth Junction) arriving at Halwill with an Up goods train from the Bude branch. Freight facilities were withdrawn from this area in the week ending 7 September 1964.

11.7.64 R.A. Lumber

'N' class 2–6–0 No. 31831 at Bude awaiting departure. The locomotive shed and water tank are on the right.

*c.* 1960 Lens of Sutton

'N' class 2–6–0 No. 31845 (72A Exmouth Junction) at Ashwater with an Up Wadebridge freight. The route code is unusually indicated with one lamp and one disc.

*c.* 1960 Lens of Sutton

'N' class 2–6–0 No. 31855 (83D Exmouth Junction) at Egloskerry with the 13.00 Padstow to Okehampton.

11.7.64 R.A. Lumber

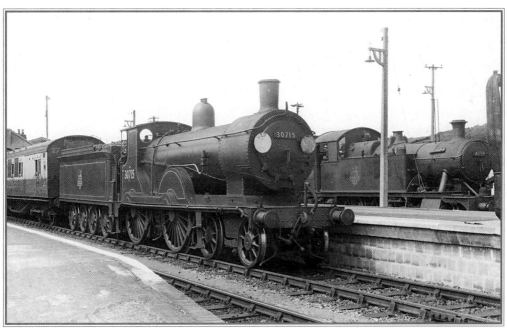

'T9' class 4–4–0 No. 30715 (72A Exmouth Junction) at Wadebridge heading a train to Okehampton. Ex-GWR '45XX' class 2–6–2T No. 4559 is in charge of a train to Bodmin Road.

25.6.65 the Revd Alan Newman

'N' class 2–6–0 No. 31847 at Wadebridge on a Down train to Padstow, awaiting '45XX' class 2–6–2T
No. 4565 with a WR train to Bodmin Road to clear the single line.

25.8.60 R.A. Lumber

The three-cylinder 'U1' class 2–6–0 No. 31903 heads an Up passenger train at Padstow.

*c.* 1960 Lens of Sutton

Ex-S&DJR Class 4F 0–6–0 No. 44558 being turned at Bath Green Park. Beyond is BR Standard Class 9F 2–10–0 No. 92214.

7.6.64 Author

Class 3F 0–6–0T No. 47552 in the MR engine shed at Bath Green Park fitted with a snow plough.

7.6.64 Author

BR Standard Class 5MT 4–6–0 No. 73047 tackles the 1 in 50 climb out of Bath as it crosses the Lower
Bristol Road. The pipe beside the bridge girders carries water from Devonshire Tunnel to Bath loco shed.

*c.* 1962 J. Hobbs

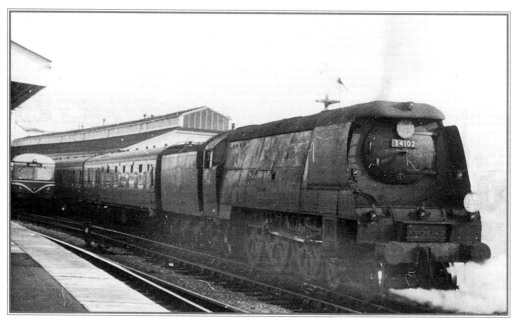

Due to a landslip at Midford, the Up 'Pines Express' headed by 'West Country' class Pacific No. 34102
*Lapford* is diverted from its usual route and travels via Salisbury and Bath Spa instead of Green Park.
A Swindon three-car 'Cross-country' DMU stands on the centre road to let it pass.

5.12.60 Author's collection

BR Standard Class 4MT 4–6–0 No. 75002, with the 3.20 p.m. Bath to Templecombe passenger train, climbs through Lyncombe Vale, Bath prior to entering the mile-long Combe Down tunnel.

10.5.62 Author's collection

Midford signalman Harry Wiltshire receives the single line tablet from the fireman of a Down train. The locomotive, Ivatt Class 2MT 2–6–2T No. 41283, is probably working the 18.05 Bath Green Park to Binegar.

*c.* 1965 C. Steane

Midford signalman Percy Savage holds up a S&D Pilotman armband, here used to hold documents. In the event of a tablet being lost, or a malfunction of Tyer's apparatus, pilotman working was instituted. Instead of a train having a tablet as authority to proceed on a single line, the pilotman aboard gave that authority.

February 1966 C. Steane

BR Standard Class 5MT 4–6–0 No. 73001 approaches Midsomer Norton up the 1 in 50 bank from Radstock with the 09.50 Bath to Bournemouth Central, Bournemouth West having closed the previous day.

5.10.65 the Revd Alan Newman

Class 3F 0–6–0T No. 47496 at Masbury Summit after banking from Radstock. The hook used by the guard to detach the engine from the van is suspended from the smokebox handrail. Note that No. 47496 has a plain three-link, and not screw, coupling.

5.9.60 Author

Class 8F 2–8–0 No. 48706 and BR Standard Class 4MT 2–6–4T No. 80043 at Evercreech Junction with a Stephenson Locomotive Society special on the last day of S&D working. No. 48706 is being watered. No. 48706 was built by the SR at Brighton in 1944, worked on the LNER as that company's No. 7652 and subsequently re-numbered 3101 and 3501 before eventually arriving on the LMS.

6.3.66 C. Steane

Class 4F 0–6–0 No. 44102 stands at Wincanton with an Up passenger train.

*c.* 1960 Lens of Sutton

Ivatt Class 2MT No. 41291 is being coaled by crane at Templecombe. Note the whitewashed turntable pit to help prevent locos or people falling in.

6.12.65 the Revd Alan Newman

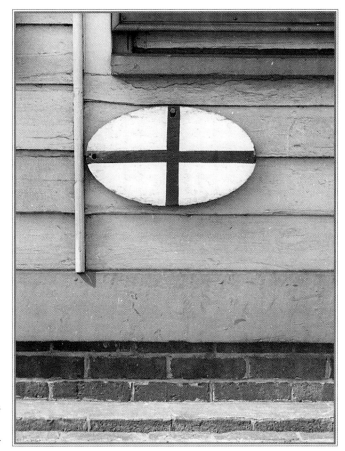

The lineman sign at Henstridge signal-box. Hung horizontally it indicated all was well; hung vertically meant the travelling lineman was required. On the reverse it was black and hung horizontally indicated the signal lineman was required, and if vertically, both linemen required. Its use was discontinued about 1930.

4.5.63 Author

BR Standard Class 9F 2–10–0 No. 92220 *Evening Star* (now preserved by the National Railway Museum) leaves Shillingstone with a Bournemouth West to Bath Green Park train.

30.9.63 the Revd Alan Newman

BR Standard Class 9F 2–10–0 No. 92220 *Evening Star* leaves Blandford Forum with a Bournemouth West to Bath Green Park train.

30.9.63 the Revd Alan Newman

Southern and L. M. S. Railway Companies'
## Somerset and Dorset Joint Line.

# WILFUL DAMAGE.

# £2 REWARD

The above Reward will be paid to any person giving such information as will lead to the discovery of the person or persons causing damage to the Fittings and Interior of **Somerset and Dorset Joint Line Carriages.**

**BY ORDER.**

An S&D notice issued in December 1924.

Author's collection

# BRANCH LINES: LSWR/SR

The LSWR branch lines in the West of England tended to be short: Yeovil Junction–Town; Chard Junction–Chard; Axminster–Lyme Regis; Seaton Junction–Seaton; Sidmouth Junction–Sidmouth; Exeter–Exmouth; Plymouth–Turnchapel and Bere Alston–Callington falling within this category. It was often the custom for a main line station to be called the junction for the branch terminus rather than the name of the local village. Where traffic and gradients permitted, these branch lines were ideal for steam railmotors, or push-pull trains in later years. The Exmouth line and the Gunnislake part of the former Callington branch are the only ex-SR branches in the West of England still carrying regular passenger trains and are valuable in providing an alternative to crowded roads. Two stations on the Exmouth branch are of particular interest: one being Lympstone Commando opened on 2 May 1976 to serve the Royal Marines Centre exclusively, and Digby & Sowton opened on 23 May 1995 to serve a park-and-ride car park, industrial estate and supermarket.

Many of the LSWR branch lines in the West of England had some unique and interesting feature. For many years the Lyme Regis line could only be worked satisfactorily by Adams' 4–4–2T engines, this type alone having sufficiently light axle load and being capable of working over the sharp curves. The three members of the '415' class retained for use on the branch outlasted their sisters by thirty-four years. Similarly, three Beattie 2–4–0 well tank engines, whose design dated back to 1862 and the majority of which were withdrawn in the 1890s, ran on the Wenford Bridge line until 1962. The Seaton branch was interesting for the fact that in association with the railway, in 1877 a road bridge and toll house were built of concrete, the latter reputed to be the oldest in England executed in that material. Although the branch closed in 1966, four years later a 2 ft 9 in gauge tramway opened on part of its roadbed, the line subsequently extended to Colyton.

The junction station for Sidmouth experienced an unusual number of name changes. Opened as Feniton, it became Ottery & Sidmouth Road the following year, then Feniton for Ottery St Mary, followed by Ottery Road. With the opening of the branch its name changed again to Sidmouth Junction. It closed when branch passenger services were withdrawn in 1967 but re-opened as Feniton in 1971. When the Sidmouth Railway was first planned in 1861 a crafty deception took place. The fact that shareholders were divided into two classes was unknown except to a few. Class A included local residents and Class B comprised those in London. Calls for money were only made on Class A!

The Exmouth line was probably the only one to have experienced the embarrassment of the guest of honour actually forgetting to turn the first sod. The Honourable Mark Rolle was supposed to have carried out the ritual, but arriving two hours late, he left his carriage and went straight to the feast, leaving the ceremony to be carried out by the company chairman. When lifting the turf the latter snapped the spade handle and had to complete the task with his hands. The opening dinner was just as memorable – one of the speakers advocated free trade, was pelted with orange peel by political rivals and a fight ensued. Exmouth has had no fewer than three stations. The original building was converted from two private houses. In 1924 this was replaced by an imposing four-platform station, while the third was a rather less imposing structure opened in 1976.

The Callington branch began as a 3 ft 6 in gauge mineral railway from Calstock Quay, subsequently converted to standard gauge with an extension opened from Calstock to the Exeter–Plymouth main line at Bere Alston. On 7 November 1966 the branch was cut back to make Gunnislake the terminus.

The North Devon & Cornwall Junction Light Railway between Torrington and Halwill Junction was the last new line of any length to be built in Devon. Although the first sod was cut on 30 June 1922, the very wet summers of 1923 and 1924 delayed construction and the line was not opened until 27 July 1925. Worked by the SR, it was nominally independent until nationalization in 1948.

The cost of a 19-mile-long standard gauge line over the hilly terrain between Barnstaple and Lynton would have been prohibitive, but a narrow gauge of 1 ft 11½ in reduced costs by two-thirds as sharper curves permitted it to follow the contours. When the line opened on 16 May 1898 the company found that the three 2–6–2Ts were insufficient. British builders could not supply owing to a strike coupled with an ordering boom, so a Baldwin 2–4–2T was purchased from the USA. In 1923 the SR bought the line, purchased a new engine and generally refurbished the railway. Despite these improvements, the line was unable to compete with the growth of road traffic and the line closed in 1935. Had it been able to continue for a further fifteen years it could well have been a candidate for preservation. The Lynton & Barnstaple Railway was unusual in that dry summers caused a grave shortage of water at Lynton station and passengers were asked to refrain from using the lavatories. In the railway's first years an early environmentalist, the Reverend J.F. Chanter of Parracombe, scattered flower seeds from a carriage window to help beautify the scars caused by construction.

Not an LSWR line, but located within its territory, was the independent Bideford, Westward Ho! & Appledore Railway, probably unique among railway companies in having an exclamation mark in its name. The village of Westward Ho! was named after Charles Kingsley's novel in order to promote the area as a holiday resort. Before opening, the company was taken over by the British Electric Traction Company. The line was inaugurated between Bideford Quay and Northam on 24 March 1901 and the extension to Appledore was first used by the public on 1 May 1908. The three 2–4–2T engines normally hauled one coach, but a second was added during the summer months when traffic was a little heavier. As the locomotives worked on a public road at Bideford, their motion was enclosed. There was no means of turning the engines, and when delivered one faced Bideford and the other two faced Westward Ho! and remained thus for all their life on the railway. A unique feature for an English standard gauge line was a single central buffer at the end of each vehicle. After only sixteen years' service the little-used line closed on 27 March 1917, the track having been requisitioned by the Government. The three locomotives were removed by means of temporary track laid across Bideford Bridge to give access to the LSWR.

At Bournemouth West BR Standard Class 4MT 2–6–0 No. 76026 with the 1.10 p.m. Bournemouth West
to Bristol Temple Meads and 'U' class 2–6–0 No. 31614 heading the 1.18 p.m. Bournemouth West to
Wimborne and Salisbury.

1.6.63 Author

'M7' class 0–4–4T No. 30056 approaches Bournemouth West with the 12.08 p.m. from Brockenhurst and
passes BR Standard Class 4MT 2–6–0 No. 76026 working the 1.10 p.m. Bournemouth West to Bristol
Temple Meads. The 'M7' carries no headlamps or discs. The Westinghouse pump for working the control
gear of the push-pull train is on the side of the smokebox.

1.6.63 Author

'M7' class 0–4–4T No. 30108 at Swanage with the 5.40 p.m. to Wareham. The route code Swanage to Wareham is a single disc or lamp in the centre of the buffer beam. The lamp above the left hand buffer is a rear lamp as the engine has just pushed the coaches from Swanage.

13.7.63 E. Wilmshurst

'02' class 0–4–4T No. 212 at Easton with a train to Weymouth. At least four of the coaches are 'gated' stock. The branch was operated jointly with the GWR.

c. 1932 Lens of Sutton

AC Cars railbus W79975 approaching Yeovil Junction from Yeovil Town.

2.4.65 the Revd Alan Newman

'54XX' class 0–6–0PT No. 5410 at Yeovil Junction on the auto service from Yeovil Town station. Although originally an LSWR service, latterly it was worked by the WR.

13.4.63 R.A. Lumber

Adams '0415' class 4–4–2T No. 30583 (72A Exmouth Junction) displays a good head of steam ready for the climb out of Axminster. In the background are cattle pens, a cattle wagon and a large goods shed. No. 30583 was sold by the LSWR to the Government in 1917 and later bought by the East Kent Railway. As only engines of this class were found satisfactory for working the Lyme Regis branch and an additional one was required, the SR purchased it from the EKR for £120 in 1946. It was withdrawn by BR in 1961 and is preserved on the Bluebell Railway.

*c.* 1960 R.J. Cannon/C.G. Maggs's collection

Adams '0415' class 4–4–2T No. 30583, en route from Axminster to Lyme Regis, eases its train round one of the tight curves.

*c.* 1960 R.J. Cannon/C.G. Maggs's collection

'M7' class 0–4–4T No. 30105, lettered 'British Railways', shunts a two-coach set and four milk tank wagons near the creamery at Seaton Junction.

18.7.48 South Western Circle Wessex Collection

'King Arthur' class 4–6–0 No. 30755 *The Red Knight* waits at Seaton Junction while the Up 'Devon Belle' passes headed by 'Merchant Navy' class Pacific No. 35009 *Shaw Savill*. No. 35009 is preserved.

*c.* 1950 Lens of Sutton

'M7' class 0–4–4T No. 30048 at Seaton with the air-worked push-pull control gear prominent in front of the side tank.

*c.* 1960 Lens of Sutton

Ex-GWR '8750' class 0–6–0PT No. 4666 at Tipton St John's on the return of a Locomotive Club of Great Britain special to Sidmouth. An Ivatt Class 2MT 2–6–2T stands on the other road.

28.2.65 Author's collection

BR Standard Class 3MT 2–6–2T No. 82010 (72A Exmouth Junction) blows off at East Budleigh with a train to Exmouth. The station is now a private house.

*c.* 1962 Lens of Sutton

Trains to and from Exmouth cross at Littleham. 'M7' class 0–4–4T No. 376 is on the Up train.

30.5.36 S.W. Baker

'M7' class 0–4–4T No. 30667, with ash wagon behind, outside Exmouth shed. The water column on the far left is stoutly built.

29.8.57 South Western Circle Wessex Collection

'M7' class 0–4–4T No. 30676 at Exmouth with an Exeter train.

*c.* 1952 M.E.J. Deane

'Skipper' railcar 142019 in chocolate and cream livery at Morchard Road working the 12.33 Barnstaple to Exmouth. The four-wheeled vehicles first appeared in May 1986, but, as they were not satisfactory for working all Devon and Cornwall branches, from October 1987 they were transferred to Manchester and Leeds.

8.8.86 Author

'M7' class 0–4–4T No. 670 and No. 30321 at Barnstaple double-head a goods train to Bideford.

13.5.50 J.H. Bamsey

At Barnstaple Junction Ivatt Class 2MT 2–6–2T No. 41248 shunts stock of the 16.40 from Torrington. No. 41248 is very dirty – both number and BR insignia are invisible and it carries no lamps or discs. To the left, North British diesel-hydraulic D6328 awaits the Torrington portion of the 10.15 Waterloo to Ilfracombe.

27.6.64 R.A. Lumber

1 ft 11½ in gauge Manning Wardle 2–6–2T No. 760 *Exe* at Lynton about to depart for Barnstaple.

1929 C.T. Standfast

Ivatt Class 2MT 2–6–2T No. 41298 having its tanks replenished at Hatherleigh while taking a mixed goods from Torrington to Halwill.

*c.* 1962 Lens of Sutton

Ivatt Class 2MT 2–6–2T No. 41249 just arriving at Halwill with the 08.52 from Torrington.

18.7.64 R.A. Lumber

'02' class 0–4–4T No. 30225 (72D Plymouth Friary) at Bere Alston with a train for Callington.

c. 1955 Lens of Sutton

'02' class 0–4–4T No. 30192 at Calstock working Set No. 15 from Callington to Bere Alston.

28.6.56 J.H. Alston

'O2' class 0–4–4T No. 30216 (72D Plymouth Friary) outside the engine shed at Callington. An ash wagon stands on the left.

5.8.51 J.H. Bamsey

At Wadebridge: ex-GWR '45XX' class 2–6–2T No. 4559 on a train to Bodmin Road and ex-SR 'T9' class 4–4–0 No. 30709 en route to Exeter Central.

c. 1954 P.Q. Treloar

'02' class 0–4–4T No. 30200 (72F Wadebridge) leaves Wadebridge for Bodmin North. The roof of the coal stage can be seen to the right.

25.6.55 the Revd Alan Newman

'45XX' class 2–6–2T No. 5502 at Padstow with the 9.08 a.m. for Bodmin Road.

7.6.49 R.J. Buckley

'0298' class 2–4–0WT No. 30586 (72F Wadebridge) near the old coaling stage at Wadebridge. The brake van, left, is marked 'Not in Common Use' and 'To work between Bodmin, Wadebridge & Padstow'.

31.7.54 Author's collection

AC Cars railbus W79978 at Boscarne Exchange Platform viewed from a Bodmin Road to Padstow train. Notice the economically built rail level platform and the folding steps to give access. The station's sole purpose when it opened in 1964 was to exchange passengers between the Bodmin North and Bodmin Road branches. Note the clay wagons on the branch. W79978 is preserved on the Colne Valley Railway.

9.8.66 Author

'0298' class 2–4–0WT No. 30587 (72F Wadebridge) at Dunmere Halt. Note the three-link, and not screw, coupling. No. 30587 is preserved on the South Devon Railway.

7.8.52 Author

'8750' class 0–6–0PT No. 4694 and SR Set No. 24 at the former SR station Bodmin North.

c. 1955 Lens of Sutton

A 2–4–0T on the standard gauge Bideford, Westward Ho! & Appledore Railway. The motion is enclosed as the public road was used for the first section out of Bideford. Behind is a teak coach with steps to give access from ground level.

*c.* 1901 Author's collection

A 2–4–0T being taken across Bideford Bridge on a specially laid temporary track following the closure of the Bideford, Westward Ho! & Appledore Railway.

1917 Author's collection

# SELECT BIBLIOGRAPHY

Baker, S.K. *Rail Atlas of Great Britain & Ireland*, Yeovil, OPC, 1996

Biddle, G. and Nock, O.S. *The Railway Heritage of Britain*, London, Michael Joseph, 1983

Body, G. *Railways of the Southern Region*, Cambridge, PSL, 1984

——. *Railways of the Western Region*, Cambridge, PSL, 1983

Bradley, D.L. *LSWR Locomotives*, Didcot, Wild Swan, 1985–9

Bradshaw *Railway Guide 1887; 1910; 1922; 1938*, Newton Abbot, D & C

——. *British Rail Main Line Gradient Profile*, Shepperton, Ian Allen, n.d.

——. *British Railways Pre-grouping Atlas & Gazetteer*, Shepperton, Ian Allen, 1976

Clark, R.H. and Potts, C.R. *An Historical Survey of Selected Great Western Stations, Vols 1–4*, Oxford, OPC, 1976–85

Clinker, C.R. *Clinker's Register of Closed Passenger Stations & Goods Depots*, Weston-super-Mare, Avon-Anglia, 1988

Cooke, R.A. *Atlas of the Great Western Railway*, Didcot, Wild Swan, 1997

Cummings, J. *Railway Motor Buses & Bus Services in the British Isles 1902–1933, Vol 2*, Oxford, OPC, 1980

Faulkner, J.N. and Williams, R.A. *The LSWR in the Twentieth Century*, Newton Abbot, D & C, 1988

Hawkins, C. and Reeve, G. *An Historical Survey of Southern Sheds*, Oxford, OPC, 1979

*The Locomotives of the Great Western Railway* (14 parts), RCTS, 1951–93

Lyons, E. *An Historical Survey of Great Western Engine Sheds, 1947*, Oxford, OPC, 1974

Lyons, E. and Mountford, E. *An Historical Survey of Great Western Engine Sheds 1837–1947*, Oxford, OPC, 1979

McDermot, E.T., Clinker, C.R. and Nock, O.S. *History of the Great Western Railway*, London, Ian Allen, 1964, 1967

St John Thomas, D. *A Regional History of the Railways of Great Britain, Vol 1, The West Country*, Newton Abbot, D & C, 1981

Williams, R.A. *The London & South Western Railway*, Newton Abbot, D & C, 1968, 1973